The Complete Forty Hadith

Fourth Revised Edition

Imam an-Nawawi

Translated by
Abdassamad Clarke

Ta-Ha Publishers Ltd.

Copyright © Abdassamad Clarke 1998

First published in Muharram 1419 AH/May 1998 CE
Second edition Muharram 1421 AH/April 2000 CE
Third edition Jumada ath-Thani 1430 AH/June 2009 CE
Fourth edition Jumada ath-Thani 1444 AH/January 2023 CE
by
Ta-Ha Publishers Ltd.
Unit 4, The Windsor Centre,
Windsor Grove,
London, SE27, 9NT, UK
www.tahapublishers.com

All rights reserved. No part of this publication may be reproduced, stored in any retrieval system, or transmitted in any form or by any means, electronic or otherwise, without written permission of the publishers.

By: Imam an-Nawawi
General Editor: Dr. Abia Afsar-Siddiqui
Translated by: Abdassamad Clarke

ISBN-13: 978 1 84200 202 5 (Hardback)

Layout by: Abdassamad Clarke

Printed by: Mega Print, Türkiye

Acknowledgements

I gratefully acknowledge the help of two scholars: Dr. Yasin Dutton of Edinburgh University, and Shaykh Ali Laraki both of whom gave generously of their time and knowledge, and unravelled several seemingly intractable problems. My thanks also to Imam Yahya Muhammad al-Hussein of Dublin for help in one particularly obstinate passage. However, since I was unable to show the complete typescript to any of the above the mistakes are mine, and the praise for its merits belongs to Allah alone.

My thanks to Dr. Abia Afsar-Siddiqui whose painstaking attention to detail as editor and proofreader has been exemplary.

Contents

Preface to the First Edition	vii
Preface to the Second Edition	viii
Preface to the Third Edition	ix
Preface to the Fourth Edition	x
Translator's Introduction	xi
Imam an-Nawawi's Introduction	1
1. Intention	5
2. The Hadith of Jibril on Islam, Iman and Ihsan	19
3. The Pillars of Islam	30
4. The Decree	33
5. Innovation	39
6. The Halal and Haram	42
7. Sincerity	47
8. Fighting	52
9. That Which I Forbid You…	55
10. Pure Wholesome Food	59
11. Doubt	63
12. Leaving What Does Not Concern One	65
13. Loving for One's Brother	68
14. The Sanctity of a Muslim's Blood	71
15. Whoever Believes in Allah and the Last Day	74
16. Do Not Become Angry	79
17. Allah has Decreed Excellence for Everything	81
18. Have Taqwa of Allah Wherever you are	83
19. Be Mindful of Allah, and He will be Mindful of you	87

20. Shame and Modesty	93
21. Istiqamah – Going Straight	95
22. The Obligations	97
23. Purity is Half of Iman	99
24. Injustice	104
25. The Wealthy and the Poor	110
26. Sadaqah	113
27. Birr and Ithm	115
28. Taqwa of Allah, Hearing and Obedience	119
29. A Comprehensive Hadith on Action	122
30. Obligations and Limits	125
31. Zuhd – Doing-Without	127
32. Causing Harm and Returning Harm	131
33. Claimants and Counter-Claimants	133
34. Seeing Something Objectionable	138
35. Brotherhood	141
36. Easing Someone's Distress	145
37. Good and Bad Actions	152
38. Obligatory and Optional Acts and Wilayah	155
39. Mistakes, Forgetfulness and Coercion	159
40. Be in the World as if a Stranger	161
41. None of You Believes until…	164
42. O Son of Adam	167
Endnotes	171

Preface to the First Edition

This translation was prepared from two editions: the first edited and annotated by Abdullah Ibrahim al-Ansari, and published by Maktabah Jiddah, the second edition from Maktabah al-Qudsi in Cairo.

The original intention of the Imam was to put these hadith and his explanatory text in front of the Muslims in a way which would be useful to them, and so for that reason we have attempted to keep this translation accurate but not academic. To that end I have not used the Arabic script at all except in two or three places in which the Imam explains Arabic words and where phonetics became more complicated than the Arabic.

As to the footnotes on the sources of the *ayat* and the hadith and for biographies of the Companions, I have largely drawn on the notes of Abdullah Ibrahim al-Ansari from the first of the above-mentioned editions.

Since much Arabic writing is concise I have added extra explanatory words in brackets [ ] if it seemed that the words were implicit in the Arabic. Sometimes I added extra explanatory comments of my own in parentheses ( ). If the matter seemed to call for extra material I gave it a footnote.

Preface to the Second Edition

In this edition we include the Arabic texts of the forty hadith. While doing that we took the opportunity to update a few matters in the text, the most substantial of which is to use the translations of the *ayat* of al-Qur'an al-Karim from *The Noble Qur'an: a new rendering of its meaning in English* by Abdalhaqq and Aisha Bewley, published by Ta-Ha Publishers. We do that because their translation is based on the meanings always understood by the Muslims as expressed in the classical *tafsir* literature. Besides that, the Bewleys are also native English speakers and this is the most readable translation of the meanings of the Qur'an and the most direct.

Preface to the Third Edition

The most substantial change to this edition has been to name the hadith, for example: 1. Intention, 2. The Hadith of Jibril on Islam, Iman and Ihsan, etc., and to use these names in the table of contents and the headers to facilitate use of the book, for it is clear that this is a book that ought to be used rather than read once and left.

For this edition, I am grateful to Mahdi Lock who pointed out the mistake that was in hadith No. 28 in both Arabic editions I consulted, in which the addition "And every error is in the Fire" had been interpolated into the Imam's narration, something only found in one narration in an-Nasa'i, which is regarded as *munkar* by the people of knowledge. See Ibn Taymiyya's explanatory footnote.

Preface to the Fourth Edition

In this edition we have replaced the graphic images of the Arabic hadith with Arabic text, and moved textual citations on bibliographic sources to the endnotes at the rear of the book, reserving footnotes for explanatory material. Footnotes are newly numbered on each page enabling the reader easily to find the explanation relating to the text being read.

Translator's Introduction

Imam an-Nawawi, may Allah be merciful to him, never intended merely to record forty hadith in a book and release them to the public. The book which he wrote was his collection of forty-two hadith together with the absolute minimum of *fiqh* and linguistic commentary which he felt necessary for people not to misunderstand the import of these hadith. Ibn 'Uyaynah said, "Hadith are misleading except to those who have *fiqh*." Ibn Wahb said, "Every man of hadith who has no imam in *fiqh* is astray. If Allah had not rescued us by Malik and al-Layth we would have gone astray."

It is clear from reading the hadith literature that the Companions, who were pre-eminently men of *fiqh*, received their Islam by means of what we would call *'taqlid'* which continued to be the means of Islam's transmission from one generation to the next. *Taqlid* is that people see with the eyes of the heart something so overwhelmingly clear that they imitate it, whether consciously or unconsciously. While this is not a decision to abandon the intellect, this word is usually translated pejoratively as 'blind imitation'. Many modern Muslims imagine that we have a wisdom superior to that because of living in a 'more enlightened' techno-scientific age. We place that concept in inverted commas because our measure of all enlightenment is the noble conduct of the Messenger of Allah ﷺ and his Companions in Madinah, a measure which shows this age to be one of the most barbaric there has ever been.

Imam Malik is reported to have said, "Only that which was effective for the first of this community will be effective for the last of it." For the Companions the encounter with the Prophet ﷺ was so extraordinary that they modelled themselves entirely upon him, sometimes even in the smallest customs and actions. As every parent witnesses, that is a major part of the process by which children learn to become adult human beings. It is from the very essence of the human being. Knowledge is not merely sets of propositions, and transmission is not just to convey those propositions to another.

This is not to denigrate the author of this book or any of the noble transmitters of traditional knowledge of this Muslim community. If we were to examine the lives of the great people of knowledge of our community we would find them to have been overwhelmed by the luminous characters and behaviour of the men and women from whom they learnt. For if the sciences have not illuminated their transmitters there is little point in transmitting them.

Thus we find Imam Malik, may Allah be merciful to him, saying, "Knowledge is a light which Allah places where He will; it is not much narration." We must accept this from Malik since his capacity for accurate narration of hadith is not in doubt, but here he is calling us to something beyond texts and certainly beyond *isnads*.

The unique achievement of the Prophet ﷺ unparalleled in all history before or since, is to have transformed the lives and practice of the elite and the ordinary people of an entire city, and from there to have transformed Arabia and the world. That miracle continues in our time. Yet Madinah was the core group, trained, educated and civilised by the last of the Messengers ﷺ.

Translator's Introduction

The next generations learnt their Islam as a generation from the Companions ﷺ. That transmission was most concentrated and authentic in Madinah. *'Amal* is the term which denotes the actual practice of the people of Madinah. The Companions transmitted it to the Followers, and they to the Followers of the Followers. All of these generations further enriched the record of the practice by their intelligent resolution of new issues in accordance with their profound knowledge of the Book and the Sunnah. Most significantly, that record includes their mode of transacting commercially without usury, the knowledge of which sustained and enriched Muslim culture for centuries and is desperately needed by the world today. The practice of the people of Madinah of those first generations is itself the best evidence of the Sunnah because it is like a *mutawatir* hadith which has been transmitted by huge numbers of reliable people of one generation to equally large numbers of reliable people of the next. In this age the best result expected of the culture of the solitary narrator is the well-meaning 'good Muslim' who is himself only too aware that he is ineffectual.

Malik, along with his pre-eminence as a narrator of hadith, recorded the *'amal* – the practice – so that it might be a wellspring for civilisations to come, as it has been and as it will continue to be insha'Allah. These hadith from the noble Imam an-Nawawi, may Allah be merciful to him, make most sense when set within the *'amal* of a dynamic and resurgent Islam like jewels in the bezel of the ring.

Two further matters in particular need to be clarified, as they constitute two of the warp threads on which the weft of this text is woven and thus all of Islam. First is the issue of *sadaqah*. The worst translation of this word is the Christian 'charity'. It is a salutary lesson for those Muslims rushing to embrace the Jews and Christians as brothers from the 'Abrahamic and monotheistic

xiii

faiths' – an abhorrent concept covering over the Jews' crimes of slandering and murdering the prophets and men of Allah, and the Christians' idolisation of Sayyiduna 'Isa ﷺ – that over a century ago a non-Muslim, the German philosopher Nietzsche, showed how terminally sick Judaeo-Christian culture is. Nietzsche called for a revaluation of all values. In his most thorough statement of that analysis, *The Antichrist*, he had also begun to declare that Islam does not share in that degeneracy. Perhaps if he had been granted more years of sanity by the grace of Allah he might have come to see that Islam is itself the very revaluation of all values for which he had called. However, we have been disappointed in some of our early translators into English who went out of their way to prove that Islam is absolutely acceptable to the Jews and the Christians. Thus these translators have wherever possible taken hold of Christian ecclesiastical language to translate the classic texts of Islam. Al-hamdulillah, more recent translators have accepted that key Arabic terms are untranslatable and that with the increasing familiarity with Arabic of English-speaking Muslims it is simplest to leave words like *'deen'*, for example, rather than choosing 'religion'.

However, with a word such as *'sadaqah'*, we must remove a misunderstanding that now adheres to the Arabic word itself. That is that, in current usage, *sadaqah* is used for the extra optional acts of generosity after the payment of *zakah*. Even a slight acquaintance with our heritage of *tafsir* and *fiqh* quickly disabuses us of this erroneous notion. *Sadaqah* is the entire zone which encompasses the obligatory *zakah*, the optional extra acts of giving, and other acts such as establishing *awqaf* endowments, but it is very often used exclusively for *zakah* itself. It is used in these forty-two hadith both in the sense of *zakah* and extra acts of generosity.

This is of importance to us in this age because, properly

Translator's Introduction

speaking, the pillar of *zakah* does not exist. That is for a number of reasons. The first reason is that *zakah* is not a charity. It is certainly a noble intention to pay from one's earnings in order to discharge the obligation that one owes to Allah, but something more is called for – a striving to recreate the authentic form of *zakah*. *Zakah* is not a voluntary giving to the poor, but rather it is an obligation of Islam. It is collected by the imams – i.e. the *khalifah* and the amirs of the Muslims – by force if necessary. A man may be fought and killed for refusing to pay the *zakah* as the Imam states so unequivocally.

The second reason is that the *zakah* can only be taken in something real which is itself *halal* and from a *halal* economy; it must be paid in gold, silver, cattle, or grains, etc. If the entire economy is based on usurious instruments, what *zakah* is possible?[i] I must refer the reader to the works of Umar Ibrahim Vadillo, particularly *The Return of the Gold Dinar*, for a thorough exposition of this matter. However, in summary it is that the banknote and other credit instruments are entirely usurious even before we consider the matter of interest, and may not be used to pay *zakah*.

Let us not be sidetracked into the fruitless debates of amateur *'ulama* which so plague our age. Let us instead be a little political. All these instruments are entirely the creation of the enemies of Islam and are under their control. All banks, including equity banks, which are sometimes called Islamic banks, operate under usurious prerequisites that allow them to lend money created out of nothing. Thus most of the currency of the paper-money system that we use comes into circulation as a debt to the banks. Neither the banknote, a usurious instrument, nor any kind of promissory note (in Arabic called *dayn*) can be used to pay *zakah*.

---

[i] That does not mean that the pillar of *zakah* may be allowed to lapse in that case, for the leader is still obliged to collect it, and the wrong action of paying it from ill-gotten gains is on the record of the one paying it.

It is the individual obligation of every Muslim to restore that pillar, since *zakah* is an individual obligation on every Muslim man and woman. The Muslim must pay *zakah* in gold and silver. We need no argument for the above. If any argument were needed for the Dinar and Dirham, it would be sufficient to say that they were the usage of the Messenger of Allah ﷺ and of the Companions and of all the right-acting generations of Muslims up to our day, and that all the texts mention them and all of these generations paid their *zakah* with them. Banks and paper money are the invention of *kuffar* and they continue to impoverish us. The return to the Islamic Dinar as the one world currency of the Muslims is the beginning of our prosperity.

The second warp thread of our text is inextricably linked with the first: it is the matter of leadership, authority and governance. The abolition of the *khilafah* is the other great *bid'ah* of our time. It is an awkward fact of history that the very movement which is most vocal in speaking out against *bid'ah* participated treacherously with *kuffar* in the destruction of the Khalifate. The story of that event is for the first time clearly exposed in the *The Return of the Khalifate* by Shaykh Dr Abdalqadir as-Sufi, in which he also outlines the route to its revival. The restoration of the Khalifate and its amirates is an individual obligation on every Muslim. Every single Muslim is obliged to pledge allegiance to a leader, as is established in the Sunnah, and to obey him and pay his *zakah* to him. That restoration will not proceed by the erection of an Islamic State, but by the compelling imperative on each Muslim to obey one worthy to lead. This is no more complicated than the issue a group of Muslims face each prayer time; someone is always found who is most fitted to lead the prayer and everyone intuitively recognises the right man. Leadership is analogous to that. If each Muslim community accepts and affirms its natural leaders, from among the leaders of the leaders

Translator's Introduction

most assuredly an Amir for the Muslims will emerge. This is the Sunnah of the Muslims, just as representational democracy, constitutionalism and republicanism are innovations of the Jews, Christians and Freemasons. We need no excuse nor proof for choosing the former and only a clear hypocrite could call us to the latter.

That is our situation. A pillar of Islam and the entire model of Islamic governance-without-state have been demolished, and it is the personal obligation of every Muslim and Muslimah to see them restored. It is not from the *fiqh* of Islam to engage in an optional act when the obligatory act has not been discharged, nor to expend energy in combating things which are disapproved when the *haram* is everywhere in evidence. It is a deviant understanding of Islam that levels all of these distinctions of *fiqh* and reduces matters to whether or not a text has an isnad. With this text we are safe, however, since it comes from a man of knowledge who was *'amil*, i.e. active in establishing the *deen*, and who was himself a noted *faqih*.

For this text to make sense it must not be modified to fit into the age in which we live as if the parameters of *kufr* were immutable, rather it must be an instrument we use in shaping the age in which we live for the sake of Allah.

Imam an-Nawawi's Introduction

Praise belongs to Allah, Lord of the Worlds, the One Who sustains the heavens and the earth, the One Who manages all the creatures, Who sent the messengers – the blessings of Allah and His peace be upon them all – to those who are charged with responsibility, to guide them and to make clear to them the laws of the *deen*, with absolute evidences and clear proofs. I praise Him for all of His blessings, and I ask Him for increase of His bounty and His generosity. I witness that there is no god but Allah alone, no partner to Him, the Overpowering One, the Nobly Generous, the Repeatedly Forgiving. I witness that Sayyiduna[i] Muhammad is His Slave and His Messenger, and His Beloved and His Intimate Friend, the best of created beings, the one who was honoured with the Mighty Qur'an – the miracle which continues with the succession of years – and with the Sunnahs which are illuminating for those who seek to take the right way, Sayyiduna Muhammad who was singled out with comprehensive words which gather many different levels

---

[i] *Sayyid* is translated in Lane's *Arabic-English Lexicon* as chief, lord and master. Sometimes a confusion arises in the use of a word such as 'lord' since that is also used to translate '*rabb*' although then in English it is conventional to use a capital letter, i.e. 'Lord'. Indeed, even the Arabic term '*rabb*' may be used linguistically for other than Allah, i.e. *rabb al-bayt* 'the man of the house', although by a specific hadith it is frowned upon for a slave to address his master as '*rabbi* – my lord' or conversely for the master to address a slave as "*abdi* – my slave'.

of meaning in them, and ease and liberality in the *deen*, the blessings of Allah and His peace be upon him and upon the rest of the prophets and messengers, and the families of all of them and the rest of the people of right action.

We have narrated from 'Ali ibn Abi Talib, 'Abdullah ibn Mas'ud, Mu'adh ibn Jabal, Abu'd-Darda', Ibn 'Umar, Ibn 'Abbas, Anas ibn Malik, Abu Hurairah and Abu Sa'id al-Khudri ﷺ through many different paths and varieties of narrations, that the Messenger of Allah ﷺ said, "Whoever preserves forty hadith for my Ummah in the affair of their *deen*, then Allah will raise him up on the Day of Rising in the company of the people of *fiqh*[i] and the people of knowledge;" and in the narration of Abu'd-Darda', "And I will be for him on the Day of Rising an intercessor and a witness;" and in the narration of Ibn Mas'ud, "It will be said to him 'Enter through whichever door of the Garden you will;'" and in the narration of Ibn 'Umar, "He will be recorded in the company of the people of knowledge and gathered in the company of the *shuhada*[ii]." Those who memorise hadith agree that it is a weak hadith even though it is narrated through many different paths.

The people of knowledge ﷺ have compiled innumerable books in this area. The first person that I know to have compiled in this area was 'Abdullah ibn Mubarak, then later Ibn Aslam at-Tusi the lordly man of knowledge, then later al-Hasan ibn Sufyan an-Nasa'i and Abu Bakr al-Ajuri, Abu Bakr Muhammad ibn Ibrahim al-Asfahani, ad-Daraqutni, al-Hakim, Abu Nu'aym, Abu 'Abd ar-Rahman as-Sulami, Abu Sa'id al-Malini, Abu 'Uthman as-Sabuni, Abdullah ibn Muhammad al-Ansari, Abu Bakr

---

[i] *Fiqh* is discrimination, the ability to discern what is obligatory, recommended, permitted, disapproved, and forbidden. Its root meaning is 'understanding' and it is used in this way in the Noble Qur'an.

[ii] *Shuhada*' 'the witnesses' are first and foremost those who die fighting in the way of Allah, although other categories are mentioned in hadith. They pass straight to the Garden at death and do not await the Resurrection or the Reckoning.

Imam an-Nawawi's Introduction

al-Bayhaqi, and a whole lot of other people of the first and later generations who cannot be enumerated.

I sought the choice of Allah [through the *du'a* known as *istikharah*] as to the matter of collecting forty hadith, modelling myself on the noted people of knowledge and guardian memorisers of Islam. The people of knowledge are unanimously agreed that it is permissible to act upon a weak hadith in the excellences of actions.[i] However, along with that I do not depend on this hadith, but rather on his ﷺ saying in the *sahih* hadith, "Let whoever of you witnesses convey it to those who are absent;" and his ﷺ words, "May Allah illuminate a man who hears my words and keeps them in mind and then conveys them just as he heard them."

Among the people of knowledge there are those who collected forty hadith on the principles of the *deen*, some of them on the derivative rulings, some on *jihad*, some on *zuhd* – doing-without, some on courtesies, some of them on public addresses, all of which are worthy purposes, may Allah be pleased with those who purposed them. My view was that I should collect forty hadith more important than all of that, i.e. forty hadith encompassing all of that, every one of which is one of the great principles of the *deen* and which the people of knowledge have described in such terms as "the *deen* revolves around it" or "it is a half of Islam" or "a third of it," etc. Moreover I decided to insist on these forty being *sahih*, the majority of them being from the two *sahih* books of al-Bukhari and Muslim, and that I should mention them without their chains of transmission in order to make their memorisation easy and to make the benefit derived from them more universal, insha'Allah, exalted is He. Then I decided to follow it up with a chapter elucidating what is hidden in their wordings. Whoever longs for the next life ought to know

---

[i] As opposed to the fundamentals and obligations.

3

these hadith because of the important matters they comprise, and that which they encapsulate which draws attention to all the acts of obedience, and that is obvious to whoever considers it. I depend upon Allah and to Him do I commit myself and His is the praise and the blessing, and by Him is success and protection from error.

الحديث الأول

عَنْ أَمِيرِ المُؤْمِنِينَ أَبِي حَفْصٍ عُمَرَ بْنِ الخَطَّابِ ﷺ قَالَ: سَمِعْتُ رَسُولَ اللهِ ﷺ يَقُولُ:

إِنَّمَا الأَعْمَالُ بِالنِّيَّاتِ وَإِنَّمَا لِكُلِّ امْرِئٍ مَا نَوَى، فَمَنْ كَانَتْ هِجْرَتُهُ إِلَى اللهِ وَرَسُولِهِ فَهِجْرَتُهُ إِلَى اللهِ وَرَسُولِهِ، وَمَنْ كَانَتْ هِجْرَتُهُ لِدُنْيَا يُصِيبُهَا أَوِ امْرَأَةٍ يَنْكِحُهَا فَهِجْرَتُهُ إِلَى مَا هَاجَرَ إِلَيْهِ.

رَوَاهُ إِمَامَا المُحَدِّثِينَ : أَبُو عَبْدِ اللهِ مُحَمَّدُ ابْنُ إِسْمَاعِيلَ بْنِ إِبْرَاهِيمَ بْنِ المُغِيرَةِ بْنِ بَرْدِزْبَهْ البُخَارِي وَأَبُو الحُسَيْنِ مُسْلِمُ ابْنُ الحَجَّاجِ بْنِ مُسْلِمٍ القُشَيْرِي النَّيْسَابُورِي : فِي صَحِيحَيْهِمَا اللَّذَيْنِ هُمَا أَصَحُّ الكُتُبِ المُصَنَّفَةِ.

1. Intention

The Amir al-Muminin Abu Hafs 'Umar ibn al-Khattab[i] said, "I heard the Messenger of Allah saying, 'Actions are only by intentions, and every man has only that which he intended. Whoever's emigration is for Allah and His Messenger then his emigration is for Allah and His Messenger. Whoever's emigration is for some worldly gain which he can acquire or a woman he will marry then his emigration is for that for which he emigrated.'"

The two Imams of the hadith scholars narrated it – Abu Abdullah Muhammad ibn Isma'il ibn Ibrahim ibn al-Mughirah ibn Bardizbah al-Bukhari and Abu'l-Husein

---

[i] He was the first to be titled "the Amir al-Muminin". The one who gave him the *kunyah* of Abu Hafs was the Prophet because of the severity that he saw in him. Al-Hafs is a dialect meaning "Lion". He gave him the title of "al-Farouq – the Discriminator" because he used to distinguish and discriminate between truth and falsehood. He was the first to declare his Islam openly, and by him Allah aided the *da'wah* of the Affirmed Truthful One when he said, "O Allah, strengthen Islam by the more beloved of the two men to you: 'Umar ibn al-Khattab or 'Amr ibn Hisham (Abu Jahl)."

The reason for his Islam was that when the acceptance of Islam by his sister Fatimah and her husband Sa'd ibn Zayd reached him, he intended to go and punish them, then his sister recited to him something from the Qur'an and he accepted Islam.

The Muslims greatly rejoiced in his acceptance of Islam and the Prophet gave him good news of the Garden, and bore witness for him that Allah put the truth upon his tongue and in his heart, and that shaytan fled from him. He is the best of the Companions after Abu Bakr and they agree unanimously about the great quantity of his knowledge, the strength of his intelligence and of his doing-without, his humility and gentleness towards the Muslims, and his great concern for whatever would benefit them. He has many virtues. 'Umar narrated 539 hadith from the Messenger of Allah. He lived for sixty-three years and died as a *shaheed*, stabbed by Abu Lu'lu'ah, and was buried along with the Prophet. His *khilafah* lasted ten years, six months and five nights.

Muslim ibn al-Hajjaj ibn Muslim al-Qushayri an-Naysaburi – in their two *sahih* books which are the most *sahih* books compiled.

Commentary

The hadith indicates that intention is the measure for rendering actions true, so that where intention is sound action is sound, and where it is corrupt then action is corrupt.

Wherever there is action accompanied by intention, then there are three states:

First, that one does it out of fear of Allah ﷻ and this is the worship of slaves.

Second, that one does it seeking the Garden and reward, and this is the worship of traders.

Third, that one does it out of modesty and shame before Allah ﷻ discharging the right of service and discharging [the duty of] gratitude, along with that seeing oneself falling short, and that one's heart is fearful because one does not know whether or not one's action is accepted. This is the worship of free people, and the Messenger of Allah ﷺ indicated it when 'A'ishah ؓ said to him, when he stood at night until his two feet swelled, "Messenger of Allah, why do you impose this upon yourself whilst *Allah has forgiven you your earlier errors and any later ones?*"[1] He said, "Shall I not be a grateful slave?"

If it is said, "Is it better to worship with fear or with hope?" It must be said, "Al-Ghazali said, may Allah be merciful to him, 'Worship with hope is better because hope causes love and fear causes despair.'"

There are three divisions with respect to those who are sincere. You must know that sincerity is exposed to the defect of conceit and whoever is conceited about his action then his action is invalid, as it is invalid if he is arrogantly proud. The second state is that one does that seeking both the world and the next life. One of the people of knowledge took the position that [in that case] his action is rejected and he sought a proof of that from his ﷺ words in the Lordly hadith (*hadith qudsi*), "Allah ﷻ says, 'I am the most independent of partners, so whoever does an action in which he makes other than Me a partner, then I am free of it.'"[2] This was the position that al-Harith al-Muhasibi took in the book *ar-Ri'ayah*. He said, "Sincerity is that you intend Him by obedience to Him and that you do not intend any other than Him." There are two types of showing off: first, that one only intends people by obedience to Him. The second is that one intends people and the Lord of people, and both of these invalidate action. The Hafidh Abu Nu'aym transmitted this statement from some of the first communities in *al-Hilyah*. One of them took a proof of that from His ﷻ words, *"The Compeller, the Supremely Great. Glory be to Allah above all they associate with Him."*[3] For just as He is too great to have a wife and child and a partner, He is too great to accept an action in which other than Him is made a partner. He ﷻ is Greater and Great and Supremely Great. As-Samarqandi said, may Allah be merciful to him, "Whatever is done for the sake of Allah is accepted, and whatever is done for the sake of people is rejected." An example of that is whoever prays Dhuhr, and intends by it to discharge the duty of what Allah has made obligatory upon him, but he lengthens its parts and its recitation and makes its organisation beautiful for the sake of people; the basic part of the prayer is acceptable, but its length and its beautification for the sake of people are unacceptable because he intends people by them.

Shaykh 'Izzu'd-Din ibn 'Abd as-Salam was asked about someone who prays and lengthens his prayer because of people, and he said, "I hope that his action will not be invalid." All of this is in the case where the association of partners occurs in attributes of the action. However, if it happens in the source of the action so that one prays the obligatory prayer for the sake of Allah 🕌 and for the sake of people, then one's prayer is not acceptable because of the association of partners in the very source of the action.

Just as showing off can be in an action, it can be in the abandonment of an action. Al-Fudayl ibn 'Iyad said, "Leaving an action because of people is showing off, and doing an action because of people is associating a partner with Allah, and sincerity is that Allah should protect one from both of them." The meaning of what he said, may Allah be merciful to him, is that whoever resolves on an act of worship and leaves it for fear that people may see it, then it is a form of showing off since he gave up an action because of people. However, if he gave it up in order to pray it in solitude this is recommended and desirable unless it is an obligatory prayer or an obligatory *zakah*, or he is a man of knowledge upon whom people model themselves, for being open about an act of worship in these cases is better.

Just as showing off invalidates action, so does seeking good report, which is that one does an act for Allah in solitude and then later tells people what one did. He 🕌 said, "Whoever makes others hear [of his actions] Allah will make others hear of him, and whoever makes a show [of his actions] Allah will make a show of him."[4] The people of knowledge say that if one is a man of knowledge upon whom people model themselves and one mentions it in order to encourage the listeners to action so that they might act in accordance with it, then there is no harm in it. Al-Mirzabani said, may Allah be merciful to him, "The one who prays needs four qualities so that his prayer will be raised up [to Allah]: presence of the heart, witnessing of the intellect, stillness in the basic elements and submission of the limbs. Whoever prays without the presence of heart is distracted, whoever prays without the witnessing of the intellect is forgetful, whoever prays without humility of the limbs is mistaken, whoever prays without stillness in the basic elements is uncouth, and whoever prays with all these elements has fulfilled the prayer."

By his ﷺ saying, "Actions are only by intentions", he meant acts of obedience aside from acts which are permissible. Al-Harith al-Muhasibi said, "Sincerity is not relevant for permitted actions because they are not acts of drawing near [to Allah] nor do they lead to drawing near, for example raising up buildings for no [higher] purpose other than frivolity. However, if it is for a purpose such as mosques, aqueducts and *ribat*-fortresses then they are desirable and recommended [acts and not merely permissible]." He said, "There is no sincerity in an act which is forbidden nor in something frowned upon, such as someone who looks at that which is not permitted for him to look at, claiming that he looks at it in order to reflect upon the workmanship of Allah ﷻ for example, one who looks at a beardless youth. There is no sincerity in this, indeed there is no act of drawing near [to Allah] in it at all." He said, "Truthfulness in the attribute of the slave is in the matching of the secret and the public, the outward and the inward. Truthfulness is realised by realising all of the stations and states, so much so that sincerity needs truthfulness, and truthfulness does not need anything, since the reality of sincerity is intending Allah ﷻ by the act of worship. One may intend Allah by the prayer but be neglectful of the presence of the heart in it. Truthfulness is intending Allah ﷻ by the act of worship along with the presence of the heart with Him. Every true one is sincere, but not every sincere one is true. That is the meaning of 'union and separation', since he has separated from other than Allah and united with the presence by Allah. It is the meaning of isolation from what is other than Allah and adornment with the presence before Allah ﷻ."

1. Intention

His ﷺ saying, "Actions are only by intentions" carries the possibilities of "the soundness of actions are only…" or "the rendering of actions sound…" or "the acceptance of actions…" or "the perfection of actions…". This was what Imam Abu Hanifah took, may Allah be merciful to him. One excludes from actions those of the category of removal, such as removing dirt, returning property obtained through extortion and loans, conveying a present, etc., for the soundness of these actions does not depend upon the intention having been made authentic, rather the reward for them depends upon having intended them as acts of drawing near. For example, one who feeds his animal, if he does so in obedience to the command of Allah ﷺ will be rewarded, but if he intends by it preservation of his wealth then there is no reward for that, as al-Qarafi said. The exception to that case is the horse of a man fighting *jihad*, for when he ties it up in the way of Allah, if it drinks and he did not intend to give it water he will be rewarded for that, as is narrated in *Sahih al-Bukhari*, and similarly for one's wife. Also locking the door and extinguishing the lamp upon going to sleep, if one intends by them obedience to the command of Allah one is rewarded, and if one intends some other thing, then one will not.

You must know that 'intention' is a word for 'purpose'. It is said, "May Allah intend good for you" i.e. "May He purpose it for you." Intention in the *shari'ah* is to purpose a thing coupled with the doing of it. If one purposes it and then does it later it is 'resolve'.

Intention is made a part of the *shari'ah* in order to distinguish customary actions from acts of worship, or to distinguish one act of worship from another. An example of the former is sitting in the mosque, which is customarily intended for rest but could also be meant as worship if the intention is for *i'tikaf*.[i] That which

---

[i] *I'tikaf* is retreat within the mosque in the last ten days of Ramadan.

distinguishes custom from worship is intention. Similarly one customarily intends by a complete washing of the body to clean the body, but the intention can also be as an act of worship (i.e. *ghusl*). That which distinguishes these two cases is the intention, which the Prophet ﷺ indicated when he was asked about the man who fought in order to show off, the man who fought defensively and the man who fought courageously, as to which of them is fighting in the way of Allah, exalted is He? He ﷺ said, "Whoever fights so that the word of Allah should be the uppermost then he is in the way of Allah, exalted is He."⁵

An example of the latter, which is distinguishing between the different degrees of worship, is someone who prays four *rak'ats* by which he could intend the midday prayer or sunnah prayers,ⁱ and that which distinguishes these two is the intention. Similarly, freeing a slave can be intended as an expiation for a wrong action and for other purposes such as [expiation of] vows [which have been broken] etc., and here that which distinguishes them is the intention.

Respecting his ﷺ words, "There is only for each man that which he intends", there is an indication that it is not permitted to deputise for someone else in acts of worship nor appoint someone as an agent from the same intention. The exceptions in this case are distribution of *zakah* and sacrifice of an 'Eid animal, for appointing someone as an agent is permissible in both these cases in the intention, and to slaughter [an animal for 'Eid] and to distribute [the *zakah*] along with the capability to make the intention. In the Hajj it is not permitted [to appoint someone to go in one's place] if one has the capability [of doing it oneself]. Paying a debt: as for when it is for one purpose it does not need an

---

Similarly, sitting having prayed the sunnah prayers and waiting for the obligatory prayer is an act of worship.

ⁱ Hanafis permit four *rak'ats* without a *tasleem* after the second *rak'ah* as a sunnah prayer.

intention. But if it is for two purposes such as someone who owes two thousands, one of which is for something he has pawned, and he pays a thousand and says, "I have paid it for the pawned item", then he is right. If he did not intend anything at the time he paid he may form and declare the intention after that and make it for whatever he wishes [i.e. to pay for the pawned item or just as a payment for his debt. It assumes that both debts are to the same person.] There is no other intention which we can delay until after the action and yet it remains sound except here.

His ﷺ saying, "Whoever's emigration is for Allah and His Messenger then his emigration is for Allah and His Messenger. Whoever's emigration is for some worldly gain which he can acquire or a woman he will marry then his emigration is for that for which he emigrated": the root of 'emigration' is 'flight' and 'abandoning'. The term *'Hijrah'* is used for a number of matters:

First, the emigration of the Companions ؓ from Makkah to Abyssinia when those who associated partners with Allah were harming the Messenger of Allah ﷺ so they fled from it to the Negus. This was five years after the sending [of the Messenger ﷺ], al-Bayhaqi said.

The second emigration was from Makkah to Madinah, and it was thirteen years after the sending [of the Prophet ﷺ]. It was obligatory on every Muslim in Makkah to emigrate to the Messenger of Allah ﷺ in Madinah. A group said without qualification that emigration was obligatory from Makkah to Madinah, however this is not the unqualified case, since there is no particular virtue in Madinah, and what was obligatory was the emigration to the Messenger of Allah ﷺ.

[Qadi Abu Bakr] Ibn al-'Arabi said, "The people of knowledge ؓ divided travel in the earth into flight and search, and the former sub-divides into six sub-divisions:

13

"First, going out from the abode of war to the abode of Islam, and this remains until the Day of Rising. That which ceased with the Opening [of Makkah to Islam] according to his ﷺ words, 'There is no emigration after the Opening',[6] was the emigration to the Messenger of Allah ﷺ where he was.

"Second, leaving the people of innovation. Ibn al-Qasim said, 'I heard Malik say, "It is not permitted for anyone to remain in a land in which the first community are being cursed."'[i]

"Third, leaving a land where the *haram* is predominant, since it is obligatory on every Muslim to seek the *halal*.

"Fourth, fleeing from harm to one's body. It is one of the bounties of Allah that He makes an allowance for that. If someone fears for himself in a place then Allah permits him to leave it, and fleeing with oneself will save one from that peril. The first to do that was Ibrahim ﷺ when he feared his people and said, '*I am leaving this place to follow the pleasure of my Lord.*'[7] He ﷺ says, telling of Musa ﷺ, '*So he left there fearful and on his guard.*'[8]

"Fifth, leaving unhealthy cities from fear of illness to go to a healthy land. He ﷺ permitted those suffering from a disease called *'aran*,[ii] when they found Madinah bad for their health, to leave and go to pasture-land.

"Sixth, leaving from fear of financial harm, since the sanctity of a Muslim's wealth is the same as the sanctity of his blood.

"As for the division of [travelling in] search, it sub-divides into ten sub-divisions [under two main headings]: seeking the *deen* and seeking the world. Seeking the *deen* has nine types:

"First, travelling for reflection; Allah ﷺ says, '*Have they not travelled in the earth and seen the final fate of those*

---

[i] Extremist *shi'ahs* such as the Fatimids used to pronounce curses on some of the Companions.

[ii] Pustules or possibly cracking and chapping of the skin, the former more commonly arising among camels and the latter among horses.

*before them?'*⁹ Indeed, Dhu'l-Qarnayn travelled around in the world in order to see its wonders.

"Second, the journey for Hajj.

"Third, the journey for *jihad*.

"Fourth, the journey for livelihood.

"Fifth, the journey for trade and extra earning over and above one's food, which is permissible because of His ﷻ words, *'There is nothing wrong in seeking bounty from your Lord.'*¹⁰

"Sixth, seeking knowledge.

"Seventh, intending to visit honoured places; he ﷺ said, 'Strenuous journeys are not undertaken except to three mosques.'¹¹

"Eighth, intending to go to the frontiers for *ribat*.ⁱ

"Ninth, visiting one's brothers for the sake of Allah, exalted is He. He ﷺ said, 'A man visited a brother of his in a town, and so Allah sent an angel in his path who said to him, "Where do you intend [to go]?" He said, "I am going to see a brother of mine in this town." He said, "Do you owe him any favour which you must repay him?" He said, "No, it is only that I love him for the sake of Allah, exalted is He." He said, "Then I am the messenger of Allah to you [with the message] that Allah loves you just as you love him."' Muslim and others narrated it." [This is the end of what Qadi Abu Bakr ibn al-'Arabi said.]

[Continuing the list of types of *hijrah*:]

Third, the emigration of the tribes to the Messenger of Allah

---

ⁱ Manning *ribat* fortresses on the frontiers in defence of the Muslims, and there training for war, practising *dhikr* of Allah and studying the *deen*. Said by some to be superior even to *jihad* since *ribat* is striving to defend the lives, property and honour of the Muslims whereas *jihad* is striving to spill the blood of the *kafirun*.

☙ in order to learn the laws of the *shariʿah* and then return to their people and teach them.

Fourth, the emigration of one of the people of Makkah, who became a Muslim, in order to come to the Prophet ☙ and then return to his people.

Fifth, the emigration from the countries of *kufr* to the countries of Islam for it is not desirable for a Muslim to reside in the abode of *kufr*. Al-Mawardi said, "If he acquires family and relatives, and it is possible for him to perform his *deen* openly then it is not permissible for him to emigrate, since the place in which he is has become for him an abode of Islam."

Sixth, the Muslim's forsaking (*hijrah*) his brother for more than three days without a reason in the *shariʿah*, which is disapproved of during the three days and *haram* every day beyond them, unless because of an over-riding necessity. It has been told as a story that a man forsook his brother for more than three days, so he [his brother] wrote these verses of poetry to him:

"O my master, you have done me an injustice,
   so seek from Ibn Abi Khaythamah a judgement about it,
     because he narrates from his grandfather
        that which ad-Dahhak narrated from ʿIkrimah,
   from Ibn ʿAbbas from the Chosen One,
     our Prophet who was sent with mercy,
   that a close friend's turning away from his close friend
     for more than three days, our Lord has forbidden."

Seventh, the husband's forsaking his wife if her disobedience is a fact. He ☙ said, "...*refuse to sleep with them* (lit.: *forsake them in the beds*)."[12] Of that [too] is forsaking (*hijrah*) disobedient people in place, in speech, in returning the greeting and in opening with a greeting.

Eighth, the forsaking of everything which Allah has forbidden and it is the most general and universal type of *hijrah*.

1. Intention

His ﷺ saying, "So whoever's emigration is for Allah and His Messenger" i.e. in intention and purpose "then his emigration is for Allah and His Messenger" in judgement and in *shari'ah*.

[About his saying] "Whoever's emigration is for some worldly gain which he can acquire...", they transmit that a man emigrated from Makkah to Madinah not wishing by that the excellence of emigration, but only emigrating in order to marry a woman called Umm Qays, and so he was called the Emigrant for the sake of Umm Qays. If someone says that marriage is one of the things sought of people in the *shari'ah* so why is it [here counted as] one of the requirements of the world? Then the answer is, "Outwardly he did not emigrate for her sake but for the sake of performing *hijrah*, so that when [that which] he concealed [was] the opposite of what he made known to people then he was worthy of reproach and blame." Analogous to that is someone who goes out with the apparent intention of performing the Hajj but really intends to go for trade.[i] Similar [to that is] someone who travels to seek knowledge and his purpose in that is to obtain leadership or a governorship.

From his ﷺ saying, "Then his emigration is for that for which he emigrated", it necessarily follows that there is no reward for someone whose purpose in the Hajj is trade and for visiting. The hadith has to be interpreted that if the thing which set him moving and sent him to the Hajj was only the trade [then he has no reward], but if the thing which sent him was [the desire to perform] the Hajj then he will have the reward and [he will have] the trade consequent to it, except that he will have a lesser reward than someone who brought himself out for the Hajj [alone]. If the thing which sent him out on the Hajj was both of them then it is

---

[i] Trade at Mina during Hajj after 'Arafat is permissible by the specific *ayah* of Qur'an, "*There is nothing wrong in seeking bounty from your Lord*" (Surat al-Baqarah: 198) which occurs in the midst of the *ayat* on Hajj, but the intention of going on Hajj must have been for the Hajj and not the trade.

conceivable that he will obtain the reward, since his travel was not set in motion for the sake of the world, but the opposite is also conceivable (i.e. that he has no reward), since he mixed an action for the next life with an action for the world. However, the hadith grades the judgement according to the purpose purely, and so it is not true that someone who intended both of them (the next life and the world) only intended the world, and Allah ﷻ knows best.

الحديث الثاني

عَنْ عُمَرَ بْنِ الْخَطَّابِ ﷺ قَالَ:

بَيْنَمَا نَحْنُ عِنْدَ رَسُولِ اللهِ ﷺ ذَاتَ يَوْمٍ، إِذْ طَلَعَ عَلَيْنَا رَجُلٌ شَدِيدُ بَيَاضِ الثِّيَابِ، شَدِيدُ سَوَادِ الشَّعْرِ، لَا يُرَى عَلَيْهِ أَثَرُ السَّفَرِ، وَلَا يَعْرِفُهُ مِنَّا أَحَدٌ، حَتَّى جَلَسَ إِلَى النَّبِيِّ ﷺ، فَأَسْنَدَ رُكْبَتَيْهِ إِلَى رُكْبَتَيْهِ، وَوَضَعَ كَفَّيْهِ عَلَى فَخِذَيْهِ، وَقَالَ: يَا مُحَمَّدُ أَخْبِرْنِي عَنِ الْإِسْلَامِ.

فَقَالَ رَسُولُ اللهِ ﷺ: الْإِسْلَامُ أَنْ تَشْهَدَ أَنْ لَا إِلَهَ إِلَّا اللهُ، وَأَنَّ مُحَمَّدًا رَسُولُ اللهِ، وَتُقِيمَ الصَّلَاةَ، وَتُؤْتِيَ الزَّكَاةَ، وَتَصُومَ رَمَضَانَ، وَتَحُجَّ الْبَيْتَ إِنِ اسْتَطَعْتَ إِلَيْهِ سَبِيلًا، قَالَ: صَدَقْتَ، قَالَ: فَعَجِبْنَا لَهُ يَسْأَلُهُ، وَيُصَدِّقُهُ.

قَالَ: فَأَخْبِرْنِي عَنِ الْإِيمَانِ، قَالَ: أَنْ تُؤْمِنَ بِاللهِ، وَمَلَائِكَتِهِ، وَكُتُبِهِ، وَرُسُلِهِ، وَالْيَوْمِ الْآخِرِ، وَتُؤْمِنَ بِالْقَدَرِ خَيْرِهِ وَشَرِّهِ، قَالَ: صَدَقْتَ.

قَالَ: فَأَخْبِرْنِي عَنِ الْإِحْسَانِ، قَالَ: أَنْ تَعْبُدَ اللهَ كَأَنَّكَ تَرَاهُ، فَإِنْ لَمْ تَكُنْ تَرَاهُ فَإِنَّهُ يَرَاكَ.

قَالَ: فَأَخْبِرْنِي عَنِ السَّاعَةِ، قَالَ: مَا الْمَسْئُولُ عَنْهَا بِأَعْلَمَ مِنَ السَّائِلِ.

قَالَ: فَأَخْبِرْنِي عَنْ أَمَارَتِهَا، قَالَ: أَنْ تَلِدَ الْأَمَةُ رَبَّتَهَا، وَأَنْ تَرَى الْحُفَاةَ الْعُرَاةَ الْعَالَةَ رِعَاءَ الشَّاءِ يَتَطَاوَلُونَ فِي الْبُنْيَانِ.

ثُمَّ انْطَلَقَ، فَلَبِثْتُ مَلِيًّا، ثُمَّ قَالَ لِي: يَا عُمَرُ أَتَدْرِي مَنِ السَّائِلُ؟ قُلْتُ: اللهُ وَرَسُولُهُ أَعْلَمُ، قَالَ: فَإِنَّهُ جِبْرِيلُ ﷺ، أَتَاكُمْ يُعَلِّمُكُمْ دِينَكُمْ.

رَوَاهُ مُسْلِمٌ.

2. The Hadith of Jibril on Islam, Iman and Ihsan

Umar ؓ also said, "One day while we were sitting with the Messenger of Allah ﷺ a man came up to us whose clothes were extremely white, whose hair was extremely black, upon whom traces of travelling could not be seen, and whom none of us knew, until he sat down close to the Prophet ﷺ so that he rested his knees upon his knees and placed his two hands upon his thighs and said, 'Muhammad, tell me about Islam.' The Messenger of Allah ﷺ said, 'Islam is that you witness that there is no god but Allah and that Muhammad is the Messenger of Allah, and establish the prayer, and give the *zakah*, and fast Ramadan, and perform the Hajj of the House if you are able to take a way to it.' He said, 'You have told the truth' and we were amazed at him asking him and [then] telling him that he told the truth. He said, 'Tell me about *iman*.' He said, 'That you believe in Allah, His angels, His books, His messengers, and the Last Day, and that you believe in the Decree, the good of it and the bad of it.' He said, 'You have told the truth.' He said, 'Tell me about *ihsan*.' He said, 'That you worship Allah as if you see Him, for if you do not see Him then truly He sees you.' He said, 'Tell me about the Hour.' He said, 'The one asked about it knows no more than the one asking.' He said, 'Then tell me about its signs.' He said, 'That the female slave should give birth to her mistress, and you see poor, naked, barefoot shepherds of sheep and goats competing in raising buildings.' He went away, and I remained some time. Then he said, 'Umar, do you know who the questioner was?' I said, 'Allah and His Messenger know best.' He said, 'It was Jibril who came to you to teach you your *deen*.'" Muslim narrated it.

Commentary

His ﷺ saying, "Tell me about *iman*." Linguistically, *iman* is unqualified 'affirmation', and in the *shari'ah* it is an expression denoting a particular affirmation, which is affirmation of Allah, His angels, His books, His messengers, the Last Day, and the Decree, the good and the bad of it. As for Islam, it is an expression denoting the performance of the obligatory duties, and it is compliance with [performance of] outward action. Allah ﷻ [in Qur'an] contrasts Islam and *iman* as in the hadith: Allah ﷻ says, *"The desert Arabs say, 'We have iman.' Say: 'You do not have iman. Say rather, "We have become Muslim."'"*[13] That is because the hypocrites used to pray, fast and give *sadaqah* (i.e. *zakah*) while yet denying it in their hearts, so that when they claimed *iman*, Allah ﷻ denied their claim of *iman* because of their hearts' denial, and He affirmed their claim of Islam because of their practice of it. Allah ﷻ says, *"When the hypocrites come to you ..."* up until His words ﷻ *"...and Allah bears witness that the hypocrites are certainly liars"*[i] i.e. [they are liars] in their claiming to bear witness to the message while their hearts are opposed, because their tongues do not agree with their hearts, and the precondition of witnessing to the message is that the tongue and the heart should be in agreement. Since *iman* is a precondition for the soundness of Islam, Allah singled the Muslims out from the *mu'minun*. Allah ﷻ says, *"We brought out all the mu'minun who were there but found in it only one house of Muslims."*[14] This is a homogeneous exception[ii] because of that connection there

---

[i] Surat al-Munafiqun: 1. *"When the hypocrites come to you they say, 'We bear witness that you are indeed the Messenger of Allah.' Allah knows that you are indeed His Messenger and Allah bears witness that the hypocrites are certainly liars."*

[ii] *Istithna muttasil* is homogeneous exception. The thing singled out – the Muslims – is of the same nature as the thing from which it is singled out –

2. Islam, Iman and Ihsan

is between the condition *(iman)* and that which is stipulated (Islam), and for this reason Allah ﷻ named the prayer *'iman'*. He ﷻ said, *"And Allah would never let your iman go to waste."*[15] He ﷻ said, *"You had no idea of what the Book was, nor iman"*[16] i.e. the prayer [in both *ayat*].[i]

His ﷺ saying, "And that you believe in the decree, the good and bad of it", [decree] can be with a *fathah* (a) on the [middle letter] *dal* (i.e. *qadar*) or with a *sukun* (without a vowel, i.e. *qadr*); they are two dialects. The position of the people of Truth is confirmation of the Decree. Its meaning is that Allah ﷻ decreed things before time, and He knew that they would come about at times known to Him and in places known to Him, and that they would come about according to how Allah had decreed.

Know that there are four decrees:

The first is the decree in knowledge, and for this reason it is said, "[Divine] concern is [decreed] before the condition of being a *wali*, and happiness is [decreed] before birth, and subsequent [events] are based on predispositions." Allah ﷻ says, *"Averted from it is he who is averted"*[17] i.e. he will be turned away from hearing the Qur'an and from affirming it in the world who was turned away from it before time. The Messenger of Allah ﷺ said, "Allah will not destroy anyone except someone who is to perish" i.e. someone who is written in the knowledge of Allah as someone who is to perish.

Second, the decree in the Preserved Tablet, and it is possible that this decree may be altered. Allah ﷻ says, *"Allah erases*

---

the *mu'minun*.

[i] Calling the *salat 'iman'* is equivalent to the saying, "*Iman* is a word on the tongue, affirmation in the heart and actions with the limbs." *Iman* may not be equated with 'belief' in the Christian sense since it encompasses the meaning of belief and much more. (Interestingly the English word 'belief' comes from an old root related to the word 'love' and has the sense of trusting, cherishing and holding dear.) It is clearly quite possible to have Islam without *iman*, which is to be a hypocrite, but more difficult to have *iman* without Islam.

whatever He wills or endorses it. And with Him is the Original of the Book."[18] It is narrated that Ibn 'Umar ؓ used to say in his supplication:

$$\text{اَللّٰهُمَّ إِنْ كُنْتَ كَتَبْتَنِي شَقِيًّا فَامْحُنِي وَاكْتُبْنِي سَعِيدًا}$$

"O Allah, if You have written me as grievous then erase me[i] and write me as happy."

Third, the decree in the womb, which is that the angel is ordered to write his provision, his life-span, and whether he is grievous or happy.

Fourth, the decreeing, which is the driving of decrees to their times. Allah ﷻ created good and bad, and decreed their coming to the slave at known times. The indication and proof that Allah ﷻ created good and bad are His ﷻ words, *"The evildoers are indeed misguided and insane…"* up to His words *"…measure (decree)."*[ii] This *ayah* was revealed about the Qadariyyah,[iii] and that (i.e. *'Taste the scorching touch of Saqar!'*) will be said to them in *Jahannam*. He ﷻ said, *"Say, 'I seek refuge with the Lord of daybreak, from the evil of what He has created.'"*[19] [As to] this division [of the decree], if graciousness towards a slave is obtained then it is averted from him before it reaches him. In the hadith there is that, *"Sadaqah [zakah] and joining ties of kinship repel an evil death and transform it into happiness."* In the hadith too there is that, *"Supplication and trial are between heaven and earth fighting, and supplication repels trial before it can descend."* The Qadariyyah claim that Allah ﷻ did not decree things before time,

---

[i] i.e. erase that decree.
[ii] Surat al-Qamar: 47. *"The evildoers are indeed misguided and insane, on the Day that they are dragged face-first into the Fire: 'Taste the scorching touch of Saqar!' We have created all things in due measure."*
[iii] Al-Qadariyyah are those who deny Allah's decree and believe in human free-will.

that His knowledge of them does not precede them, that they are just beginning now, that He ﷻ only knows about them after their occurrence, and they have lied about Allah – majestic is He above their lying statements and exalted is He with a great exaltedness – and these have perished. The Qadariyyah began to say in later times that the good is from Allah and the evil from other than Him, exalted is Allah above their statement. It is established as an authentic statement that he ﷺ said, "The Qadariyyah are the Magians of this community."[20] He called them Magians (Zoroastrians) because of the resemblance of their school to the school of the Magians. The dualists claim that good is from the action of light and that evil is from the action of darkness and so they become dualists. Similarly the Qadariyyah ascribe good to Allah and evil to other than Him, and He ﷻ is the Creator of good and evil.[i] Imam al-Haramayn said in the book *al-Irshad*, "Some of the Qadariyyah say, 'We are not Qadariyyah, rather you are Qadariyyah because you believe in reports which are transmitted about the decree'" and he refuted these ignorant people saying that they ascribe the decree to themselves. Whoever claims evil for his self and ascribes it to it, then it is more fitting that it should be related to him than to one who ascribes it to other than him and rejects its attribution to himself.

---

[i] There is a very strong element of dualism in Judaeo-Christian culture, i.e. the dominant world culture today, which is seen in the act of giving to satan an almost omnipotent power as the creator of evil. This has tainted the modern age, so that for example 'The Lord of the Rings' and 'Star Wars' show an ascription of 'almost divine' power to evil, with the good only just managing to overpower it. The noble Imam an-Nawawi ﷺ affirms the position of the people of *Tawhid* that Allah ﷻ is the author of good and evil, which are both tests and trials from Him, blessed is He and exalted, evil not having the absolute quality ascribed to it by some but a relative value only.

Dualistic thinking has also infected the Muslim community from the first days, for example in elements of *shi'ism*, particularly and very strikingly the thinking of Ali Shariati, and modern movements which speak using a dualistic application of the Qur'anic terms '*haqq*' and '*batil*', etc.

About his ﷺ saying, "...'Tell me about *ihsan*.' He said, '*Ihsan* is that you worship Allah as if you see Him...'", this is the station of witnessing. If one should be given the capacity to witness the King, one would be too ashamed to turn towards other than Him in the prayer and to occupy one's heart with other than Him. The station of witnessing is the station of the *Siddiqun* (the totally truthful people). We have previously had an indication of that in the first hadith.

His ﷺ saying, "...then He sees you" [i.e. to be] forgetful, if you are forgetful in the prayer and holding inner conversations with yourself in it.

His ﷺ saying, "...'Tell me about the Hour.' He said, 'The one asked about it is not more knowledgeable than the one who asks.'" Is this response because he ﷺ did not know when the Hour would be? Indeed, the knowledge of the Hour is something which Allah ﷻ alone possesses. Allah ﷻ says, *"Truly Allah has knowledge of the Hour."*[21] He ﷺ said, *"It hangs heavy in the heavens and the earth. It will not come upon you except suddenly."*[22] He ﷺ said, *"What will make you understand? It may be that the Last Hour is very near."*[23]

Whoever claims that the duration of the world is seventy thousand years and that sixty-three thousand years remain, it is a false statement which at-Tukhi related in *Asbab at-Tanzil* from some astrologers and numerologists. Whoever claims that the duration of the world is seven thousand years, is postponing the Unseen and it is not permitted to believe it.

His ﷺ saying, "... 'Then tell me about its signs.' He said, 'That the female slave should give birth to her mistress.'" *Amar* and *Amarah* (a sign) with and without *ta'* (*marbutah*) are both usages in Arabic dialects. It has been narrated both as "her lord"[i] and "her

---

[i] '*rabbaha*' – her lord' and this is an example of the linguistic use of '*rabb*' for other than Allah.

mistress". The majority say that this informs us of the plenitude of female slaves and their children [at that time], because her child from her master has the status of her master, since a man's wealth goes to his children.[i] It has been said that it refers to slave women giving birth to kings, so that she becomes one of his subjects. It is possible for it to mean that a person made his female slave pregnant with a child, then sold her,[ii] and the child grew up and bought his mother. This is one of the signs of the Hour.

His ﷺ saying, "…and you see poor, naked, barefoot shepherds of sheep and goats competing in raising buildings." Here *'alah* are the *fuqara'*[iii] (the needy) and *'a'il* is the *faqeer* (the needy one) and *'aylah* is need/poverty, and the verb is *'ala* (the past tense "he was or became needy"), *ya'ilu* (the present tense "he is needy") and *'aylah* (the verbal noun "needing"). *Ri'a* (shepherds) with the *kasrah* (i) under the *ra'* and with a *madd* [on the *alif* after the *'ayn*] – and it has also been said about it *ru'ah* with a *dammah* (u) on the *ra'* and with the increase of a *ta'* (*marbutah*) and without a *madd*[iv] – its meaning is that people of the countryside, and their

---

[i] A great many of the *khulafa'* of Islam have been the sons of slave women.

[ii] It is not permitted to sell the mother of one's children. From the *Muwatta'*, "Malik related to me from Nafi' from 'Abdullah ibn 'Umar that 'Umar ibn al-Khattab said, 'If a slave-girl gives birth to a child by her master, he must not sell her, give her away or bequeath her. He enjoys her and when he dies, she is free.'"

[iii] *Faqeer* derives from the root 'he was in need', and so the *fuqara'* are 'the needy' rather than 'the poor'. For this reason the Sufis use the term in the same sense as the Qur'anic *ayah* where Allah ﷻ says, "O mankind you are the needy ones with respect to Allah…" rather than in the sense of that category of people who are able to accept the *zakah* because of their 'poverty' i.e. their material need.

[iv] Since it is very simple in Arabic to make a mistake in writing, printing or reading, and to confuse letters from the same family such as *'ayn* and *ghayn*, Arabic scholars, when commenting on a difficult word, spell it out in just such a laborious way to make sure that no confusion can arise, specifying the letter and whether it has diacritical points, and spelling out the vowelling as well.

like of people in need and want, rise high in building, and the world is expanded for them so much that they compete boastfully with each other in construction.

His ﷺ saying, "...and he remained some time *(labitha)*", is with an 'a' on the *tha'* on the assumption that it is the third person singular ('he'), and it has been said that it is "I remained" *(labihtu)* with the addition of the *ta'* of the first person singular ('I'), and both of them are *sahih*. *Maliyya* with a *shaddah* on the *ya'* means "a long time". In the narration of Abu Dawud and at-Tirmidhi there is that he said, "After three days...." In the *Sharh at-Tanbih* of al-Baghawi there is that he said, "After three or more" and this apparently means after three nights. Apparently this contradicts the words of Abu Hurairah in his hadith, "Then later the man turned back and the Messenger of Allah ﷺ said, 'Bring the man back to me', so they went to bring him back but could see nothing. The Messenger of Allah ﷺ said, 'This was Jibril.'" It is possible to harmonise these two by saying that 'Umar ؓ was not present when the Prophet ﷺ spoke to them at that time, because he had left the gathering, and the Prophet ﷺ told those assembled there at that time and they told 'Umar three days later since he had not been present when the others were told.

In his ﷺ statement, "This was Jibril who came to teach you your *deen*" there is a proof that *iman*, Islam and *ihsan* are together called '*deen*'.

In the hadith there is proof that affirmation of the decree is obligatory, that one must give up plunging into matters, and that it is obligatory to be content with the decree. A man came to Ahmad ibn Hanbal ؓ and said, "Counsel me!" He said to him, "If Allah ﷺ has undertaken responsibility for provision then why your concern? If it is true that Allah will replace [what you spend] then why meanness? If the Garden is true why rest? If the questioning of Munkar and Nakir is true why be cheerful? If the world is evanescent why be at ease? If the reckoning is true why collect? If everything is ordained and decreed then why fear?"

A Useful Point

The author of the *Hilyat al-'Ulama* (Stations of the People of Knowledge) mentioned that the whole world is divided into twenty-five portions, five of which are by general and particular decree (*qada* and *qadar*), five by struggle and exertion, five of which are by custom and habit, five by disposition[i] and five by inheritance. As for the five of them which are by general and particular decree, they are provision, children, family, authority and life-span. The five which are by exertion are the Garden, the Fire, abstinence, horsemanship and writing. The five which are habitual are eating, sleeping, walking, marriage, and relieving oneself. The five which are by disposition are doing-without, sharpness of mind,[ii] giving, beauty and awe. The five which are inherited are goodness, continuity, liberal generosity, truthfulness and trustworthiness. None of this negates his saying, "Everything is by general and particular decree."[24] It only means that some of these things are arranged according to cause, some of them have no cause, and all of them are by general and particular decree.

---

[i] *Jawhar* – 'substance' or 'essence', or what is in-built in the person's nature, i.e. their disposition.

[ii] *Dhakah* means mental acuity. In both editions I used it was mistakenly written as *zakah*. If it is *zakah* it means 'purity' as in Surah Maryam: 11-12 "'Yahya, take hold of the Book with vigour.' We gave him judgement while still a child, and tenderness and purity from Us."

الحديث الثالث

عن أبي عبدِ الرحمنِ عبدِ اللهِ بنِ عمرِ بنِ الخطَّابِ رضي الله عنهما، قالَ: سَمِعتُ رَسُولَ اللهِ ﷺ يَقُولُ:

بُنِيَ الإِسْلامُ على خَمْسٍ: شَهَادَةِ أَنْ لاَ إِلَهَ إِلاَّ اللهُ وأَنَّ محمَّدًا رَسُولُ اللهِ، وإقامَةِ الصَّلاةِ، وإيتَاءِ الزَّكَاةِ، وَحَجِّ البَيْتِ، وصَوْمِ رَمَضَانَ.

رواه البخاري، ومسلم.

3. THE PILLARS OF ISLAM

Abu 'Abd ar-Rahman 'Abdullah ibn 'Umar ibn al-Khattab[i] ﷺ said, "I heard the Messenger of Allah ﷺ say, 'Islam is built on five: witnessing that there is no god but Allah and that Muhammad is the Messenger of Allah, establishment

---

[i] 'Abdullah became a Muslim in Makkah with his father while still young and emigrated with him to Madinah. He was one of the Companions who was learned in *fiqh*. He lived to a great age and transmitted to many of the great ones of the next generation, one of the most famous of whom was his freed slave Nafi', one of the main teachers of Malik ibn Anas ﷺ. Scholars count the *isnad*: Malik from Nafi' from Ibn Umar from the Messenger of Allah ﷺ as the 'Golden *Isnad*'. His son Salim was also one of the great *fuqaha*' of his time.

of the prayer, payment of *zakah*, Hajj of the House, and the fast of Ramadan.'" Al-Bukhari and Muslim narrated it.

Commentary

His ﷺ saying, "Islam is built on five" i.e. so whoever produces these five has completed his Islam. Just as the corners and walls complete the house, Islam is completed by its pillars which are five in number. This is 'building' in the realm of meaning whose metaphor is physical building. The basis of the metaphor is that when one of a physical building's corners or sides is in ruin then the building itself is incomplete, and it is similar for building in the realm of meaning. For that reason he ﷺ said, "The prayer is the pillar of the *deen*. Whoever abandons it has ruined the *deen*."[25] In that way it (a physical building) is analogous to it (the *deen*).

Something that has been said about building in the realm of meaning is:

> The construction of affairs, with the people of the *deen*, is as long as they are right acting,
> And if they turn away, then by the worst are they (affairs) guided.
> Men do not put chaos right if they have no leader,
> and they have no leader if ignorant ones overmaster [them].
> And a house is not built unless it has pillars,
> and it has no pillar if the pegs are not firm.

Allah struck a metaphor for the believers and the hypocrites. He ﷺ said, *"Who is better: someone who founds his building on taqwa of Allah and His good pleasure...?"*[26] wherein He compares the building of the believer to one who places his building right on the middle of a firm mountain, and He compares the building of a disbeliever to one who places his building on the edge of the crumbling bank of a sea, it having no stability, and at which the sea eats away so that the bank collapses, and thus the building collapses and falls with him into the sea, and he is drowned and enters *Jahannam*.

His ﷺ saying, "Islam is built on five…" i.e. "on" with the meaning of "with", for if that were not the case then the building would be something other than that with which it is built. If we were to interpret it according to the strict literal meaning then the "five" would be outside of Islam and that is a warped meaning. It is possible that it ("on") is with the meaning of "from" as in His ﷺ words, "…*except on* (*'ala*) *their spouses*…"[i] i.e. "…from their spouses".

The five which are mentioned in the hadith are the foundations of the building. As for the supplementary matters and things which complete [the building] they are like the rest of the duties, and the other recommended acts which are the ornamentation of the building. It has been narrated in hadith that he ﷺ said, "*Iman is more than seventy branches the highest of which is the saying 'There is no god but Allah'*" and he said, "*…and the least of which is removal of some harm from the pathway.*"[27]

He ﷺ said, "…and Hajj of the House and the fast of Ramadan", and thus it is in this narration with Hajj preceding the fast. This is according to the order in which they are mentioned but not according to their relative importance in judgement, since the fast of Ramadan is a duty before the Hajj. In other narrations the fast precedes the Hajj.

---

[i] Surat al-Mu'minin: 6. "…*those who guard their private parts – except from their wives…*". The *ayah* uses "'*ala* (on)" in the sense of "*min* (from)".

الحديث الرابع

عن أبي عبدِ الرحمنِ عبدِ اللهِ بن مسعودٍ رضي اللهُ عنه، قَالَ: حدَّثَنا رَسولُ اللهِ - وهُوَ الصَّادقُ المَصْدُوقُ:

إنَّ أحَدكُم يُجمَعُ خَلقُه في بَطنِ أمِهِ أربَعينَ يوماً نُطفَةً، ثمَّ يكُونُ عَلقَةً مثلَ ذلكَ، ثمَّ يكُونُ مُضغَةً مِثلَ ذلكَ، ثمَّ يُرسَلُ إلَيْهِ المَلَكُ، فيَنفُخ فيهِ الرُّوحَ، ويُؤمَرُ بأربَعِ كَلِماتٍ: بِكَتْبِ رِزْقِهِ، وأجَلِهِ، وعَمَلِهِ، وشَقيٌّ أم سَعيدٌ؛ فواللهِ الَّذي لا إلَهَ غيرُه إنَّ أحَدَكُم لَيَعمَلُ بِعَمَلِ أهلِ الجَنَّةِ حتَّى ما يكُونُ بينَه وبينَها إلاَّ ذِراعٌ فيَسبِقُ عَليهِ الكِتابُ فيَعمَلُ بِعَمَلِ أهلِ النَّارِ فيَدخُلها. وإنَّ أحَدَكُم لَيَعمَلُ بِعَمَلِ أهلِ النَّارِ حتَّى ما يكُونَ بينَهُ وبينَها إلاَّ ذِراعٌ

$$\text{فَيَسْبِقُ عَلَيْهِ الْكِتَابُ فَيَعْمَلُ بِعَمَلِ أَهْلِ الْجَنَّةِ فَيَدْخُلُهَا.}$$

$$\text{رواه البخاري، ومسلم.}$$

4. THE DECREE

Abu 'Abd ar-Rahman 'Abdullah ibn Mas'ud[i] ﷺ said, "The Messenger of Allah ﷺ told us – and he is the truthful one who is confirmed – 'Any one of you, his creation

---

[i] He became a Muslim very early on in Makkah, and it is said that he was the sixth to accept Islam. The cause of his Islam was that the Prophet ﷺ passed by him when he was shepherding sheep and goats for 'Uqbah ibn Abi Mu'ayt and said to him, "Boy, do you have any milk for us to drink?" He said, "Yes, but I have been entrusted [with it]." He said, "Do you have a lamb which the ram has not yet mounted?" He said, "Yes," and he brought it to him. The Prophet ﷺ rubbed its udder and supplicated and its udder filled with milk. He milked it into a vessel which Abu Bakr ﷺ brought him. Then he said to the udder, "Contract!" and it contracted, i.e. it returned to the condition in which it had been, without milk. When he saw that, he accepted Islam.

He dealt the death blow to Abu Jahl at the Battle of Badr.

Later he resided in Kufa and was the teacher there, transmitting his knowledge to them. Therefore his traditions are one of the main pillars of Hanafi *fiqh*.

He was the possessor of the Chosen One's secret, and used to say, "By Allah the One other than whom there is no god, no *ayah* from the Book of Allah has been revealed but that I know where it was revealed, and about what it was revealed. If I had known that anyone knew more about the Book of Allah than me and it had been possible to reach him by camel I would have gone to him."

848 hadith are narrated from him. He died in Madinah in 33 AH just over sixty years old, and was buried in al-Baqi'.

is gathered in the belly of his mother for forty days as a drop, then later he is a blood clot for the like of that, then later he is a morsel of flesh for the like of that. Then the angel is sent to him and breathes the spirit into him, and he is commanded with four words: with writing his provision, his life-span, his action, and whether he is happy or grievous. By Allah the One other than Whom there is no god, one of you will do the actions of the people of the Garden until there is only a cubit[i] between him and it, then the decree will overtake him, he will do the actions of the people of the Fire and thus enter it. One of you will do the actions of the people of the Fire until there only remains a cubit between him and it, then the decree will overtake him, he will do the actions of the people of the Garden and so enter it.'" Al-Bukhari and Muslim narrated it.

Commentary

The saying of 'Abdullah ibn Mas'ud, "...and he is the truthful one who is confirmed" i.e. Allah bore witness that he is the truthful one, and "confirmed" means he is trustworthy.

His ﷺ saying, "His creation is gathered in the belly of his mother", it is possible that what is meant by it is, "The water of the man and of the woman are united and the child is created from the two of them" as He ﷻ said, "...*created from a spurting fluid.*"[28] It is possible that what is meant is that he is gathered together from all of the body. That is because it is said that the [sperm] drop in the first state courses in the woman's body for forty days, which are the days of craving. After that it is collected and some of the dust of the child flows copiously over it and it becomes transformed into a clot. Then it continues in the second state and begins to grow larger until it becomes a chewed morsel

---

[i] *Dhira'* – a cubit is the length from the finger tips to the elbow.

of flesh. It has been named thus because it is the size of a piece of meat which is chewed. Then in the third state Allah fashions that morsel and creates hearing, sight, smell and the mouth in it, and He fashions the intestines within it. He ﷻ said, "*It is He who forms you in the womb however He wills.*"²⁹ When the third stage is complete, and that is forty [days], the child is four months old and the spirit is breathed into it. Allah ﷻ says, "*Mankind! if you are in any doubt about the Rising, know that We created you from dust...*"ⁱ meaning "your father Adam" "*...then from a drop of sperm (nutfah)...*" meaning his (Adam's) descendants [are created from a drop whereas Adam was created from dust] and the drop is the sperm – and its root is 'little water' and its plural in Arabic is *nitaf* – "*then from a clot of blood*" which is thick congealed blood, and that drop of sperm becomes thick blood, "*...then from a lump of flesh...*" which is a piece of meat "*...formed yet unformed*" about which Ibn 'Abbas said, "*Formed*, i.e. 'completed', and *unformed*, i.e. 'uncompleted', indeed deficient in its creation." Mujahid said, "Fashioned and unfashioned", [the latter] meaning the miscarried foetus.

Ibn Mas'ud ﷺ said, "When the drop is settled in the womb the angel takes it in his palm and says, 'O my Lord, formed or unformed?' And if He ﷻ says, 'Unformed' he casts it into the womb as blood and it does not become a person. If He says, 'Formed' then the angel says, 'Is it male or female? Is it happy or grievous? What is its provision and what is its life-span, and in which land will it die?' It will be said to him, 'Go to the Original of the Book, for you will find all of that in it.' He will go and will find it in the Original of the Book and write it until it comes to the last description of it." For this reason it is said, "Happiness is [decreed] before birth."

ⁱ Surat al-Hajj: 5. "*Mankind! if you are in any doubt about the Rising, know that We created you from dust then from a drop of sperm then from a clot of blood then from a lump of flesh, formed yet unformed...*"

4. The Decree

His ﷺ saying, "...then the decree will overtake him", i.e. that [decree] which preceded in knowledge, or that which preceded in the Preserved Tablet, or that which preceded in the belly of the mother, and we have already seen that there are four decrees.

His ﷺ saying, "...until there is only a cubit between him and it" is a metaphor by which is meant a piece of time at the end of his life; it does not literally mean a cubit and that precise amount of time, for when the disbeliever says, "There is no god but Allah, Muhammad is the Messenger of Allah" then dies, he enters the Garden. When the believer says at the end of his life the word of disbelief, he enters the Fire. In the hadith there is a proof that one must not make unequivocal statements about [anyone] entering the Garden or the Fire, even if the person does all sorts of right action or all sorts of wrong action, and that one must not depend on one's action nor be conceited about it, since one does not know what is the seal [of one's destiny]. Everyone ought to ask Allah ﷻ for a good conclusion [to their life], and seek refuge with Allah ﷻ from an evil conclusion.

If it is said, "Allah ﷻ says, 'But as for those who have iman and do right actions, We will not let the wage of good-doers go to waste,'[30] then the apparent meaning of the *ayah* is that right action from a sincere person is accepted, and that if acceptance has been obtained because of the promise of the Generous One, then he is safe by that from an evil conclusion", then the answer has two aspects, one of which is that it is conditional on acceptance and [the decree of] a good conclusion. It may also possibly mean that whoever believes and is sincere in his action will not have anything but a good conclusion [to his life] and that the evil conclusion will only be for the one who does wrong action or mixes it with right action mixed with some form of showing off or seeking reputation, and another hadith indicates this: "One of you will act with the actions of the people of the Garden as it appears to people", i.e. in that which is apparent to them of the rightness of his outward along with the corruption and foulness of his inward, and Allah knows best.

In the hadith there is a proof that it is desirable to swear an oath to emphasise a matter to people, and Allah ﷻ swore, *"By the Lord of heaven and earth, it is certainly the truth."*[31] Allah ﷻ says, *"Say, 'Oh yes, by my Lord, you certainly will be raised again! And then you will be informed about what you did.'"*[32] Allah ﷻ knows best.

الحديث الخامس

عَنْ أُمِّ المؤمنينَ أُمِّ عبدِ اللهِ عائشةَ رضي اللهُ عنها، قَالَتْ: قَالَ رَسُولُ اللهِ ﷺ:

مَنْ أَحْدَثَ فِي أَمْرِنَا هَذَا مَا لَيْسَ مِنْهُ فَهُوَ رَدٌّ.

رواه البـخاري، ومسلم. وفي رواية لمسلم:

مَنْ عَمِلَ عَمَلاً لَيْسَ عَلَيْهِ أَمْرُنَا فَهُوَ رَدٌّ.

5. Innovation

The Mother of the Believers, Umm 'Abdullah 'A'ishah[i] said, "The Messenger of Allah ﷺ said, 'Whoever introduces into this affair of ours that which is not of it,

---

[i] She is known as the *Siddiqah* – the thoroughly truthful one – and she was the daughter of the *Siddiq*, Abu Bakr ﷺ. She was given the surname of Mother of the Believers by the Qur'an which named all the wives of the Prophet thus. She was the most beloved of his wives after Khadijah ﷺ. The Prophet ﷺ married no other previously unmarried woman apart from her. She was tremendously knowledgeable in *fiqh*, characterised by doing-without in the world, generous, eloquent, and much given to fasting. The Prophet ﷺ advised us to take half of our *deen* from her.

Abu Musa al-Ash'ari ﷺ said, "No hadith ever showed us difficulty but that when we asked 'A'ishah about it we found that she had knowledge of it."

Az-Zuhri said, "If the knowledge of 'A'ishah had been gathered together

then it is rejected.'"ⁱ Al-Bukhari and Muslim related it, and in a narration of Muslim's there is, "Whoever does an act for which there is no command of ours then it is rejected."

Commentary

In his ﷺ saying, "Whoever introduces into this affair of ours that which is not of it, then it is rejected", there is an indication that if the acts of worship, *ghusl*, *wudu'*, fasting and prayer, are performed in a manner which contradicts the *shari'ah* they are returned to the one who performed them, and that which is taken by a corrupt contractⁱⁱ must be returned to its owner and not taken possession of.

He ﷺ said to someone who said to him, "My son was an employee of this one and fornicated with his wife. I have been told that my son must be stoned, so I have paid a ransom of two hundred sheep and a slave-girl for him." He ﷺ said, "The slave-girl and the sheep are rejected and returned to you."

In it there is an indication that whoever innovates something in the *deen* which does not accord with *shari'ah*ⁱⁱⁱ then its guilt is

---

and the knowledge of all the wives of the Prophet ﷺ and of all other women, 'A'ishah's knowledge would be greater."
She narrated 1,210 hadith.
She died when she was sixty-six years old and is buried in al-Baqi'.

ⁱ Rejected – *radd* also has the sense of 'returned'.

ⁱⁱ It is commonplace to regard innovations as being merely in the 'religion' which, in the post-colonial era, has been made of Islam, whereas Imam an-Nawawi clarifies that contractual matters, which include commercial transactions, have *shari'ah* forms.

ⁱⁱⁱ This phrase necessarily implies, as was the position of Imam an-Nawawi, that someone who innovates something in the *deen* which does accord with the *shari'ah* has no guilt and his action is not rejected. Of course, this is an issue only for people of knowledge with the necessary qualifications.

One of the best works on *bid'ah* is the *Ihya as-Sunnah wa Ikhmad al-Bid'ah* (Revival of the Sunnah and Destruction of *Bid'ah*) of Shaykh 'Uthman dan

5. Innovation

upon him and his action is rejected and returned to him, and that he merits the threat.

He ﷺ said, "Whoever introduces a new matter or gives shelter to an innovator then the curse of Allah be upon him."

Fodio, may Allah show him mercy, in which he says, "My purpose is not to rend those things which veil people [and their wrong actions] nor to become occupied with their defects. Whoever's purpose is to revive the Muhammadan Sunnah and to destroy shaytanic *bid'ah* will expend himself in counselling Muslims, and Allah is responsible for helping him. Whoever's purpose is to rend people's veils [over their weaknesses and wrong actions] and to become occupied with their defects, then Allah is his Reckoner and He will question him, because whoever follows up the nakedness of his brother, then Allah will follow up his nakedness and disgrace him even though right inside his own house. The believer seeks excuses for [others' behaviour] and the hypocrite follows up defects. Allah helps the slave as long as the slave helps his brother. There is in the *Muwatta'*, 'Do not look into people's wrong actions as if you were lords, but look into your own wrong actions as if you were slaves.'"

الحديث السادس

عَنْ أَبِي عَبْدِ اللَّهِ النُّعْمَانِ بْنِ بَشِيرٍ رَضِيَ اللَّهُ عَنْهُمَا، قَالَ: سَمِعْت رَسُولَ اللَّهِ ﷺ يَقُولُ:

إِنَّ الْحَلَالَ بَيِّنٌ، وَإِنَّ الْحَرَامَ بَيِّنٌ، وَبَيْنَهُمَا أُمُورٌ مُشْتَبِهَاتٌ لَا يَعْلَمُهُنَّ كَثِيرٌ مِنَ النَّاسِ، فَمَنِ اتَّقَى الشُّبُهَاتِ فَقَدِ اسْتَبْرَأَ لِدِينِهِ وَعِرْضِهِ، وَمَنْ وَقَعَ فِي الشُّبُهَاتِ وَقَعَ فِي الْحَرَامِ، كَالرَّاعِي يَرْعَى حَوْلَ الْحِمَى يُوشِكُ أَنْ يَرْتَعَ فِيهِ، أَلَا وَإِنَّ لِكُلِّ مَلِكٍ حِمًى، أَلَا وَإِنَّ حِمَى اللَّهِ مَحَارِمُهُ، أَلَا وَإِنَّ فِي الْجَسَدِ مُضْغَةً إِذَا صَلَحَتْ صَلَحَ الْجَسَدُ كُلُّهُ، وَإِذَا فَسَدَتْ فَسَدَ الْجَسَدُ كُلُّهُ، أَلَا وَهِيَ الْقَلْبُ.

رَوَاهُ الْبُخَارِيُّ، وَمُسْلِمٌ.

6. The Halal and Haram

Abu 'Abdullah an-Nu'man ibn Bashir[i] ﷺ said, "I heard the Messenger of Allah ﷺ saying, 'The *halal* is clear and the *haram* is clear and in between them there are ambivalent matters which many people do not know. Whoever guards himself against ambivalent matters has secured his *deen* and his honour. Whoever falls into ambivalent matters will fall into the *haram*, like the shepherd who shepherds [his flock] around forbidden pasturage, he is certain to pasture [his flock] in it. Certainly, every king has his forbidden pasturage. Certainly, Allah's forbidden pasturage is the things He has forbidden. Certainly in the body there is a lump of flesh which when it is sound the whole body is sound and when it is corrupt the whole body is corrupt. Certainly it is the heart.'" Al-Bukhari and Muslim narrated it.

Commentary

His ﷺ saying, "The *halal* is clear and the *haram* is clear and in between them are ambivalent matters ...". The men of knowledge differ as to the definition of the *halal* and the *haram*. Abu Hanifah said, may Allah show him mercy, "The *halal* is that for which there is a proof which shows that it is *halal*." Ash-Shafi'i ﷺ said,

---

[i] He was born at the beginning of the fourteenth month after the *Hijrah*, and his mother carried him to the Chosen One ﷺ who asked for a date and chewed it, then put it into his mouth. He was the first child born to the Ansar after the arrival of the Prophet ﷺ in Madinah. He learnt from the Prophet ﷺ when he was young and narrated what he learnt as hadith after his puberty. He was appointed amir of Kufa, he was the *qadi* of Damascus and Homs, and he was one of the most gifted of those who gave the *khutbah*.

114 hadith have been narrated from him. He was assassinated at the age of sixty-four.

"The *haram* is that for which there is a proof that shows it is *haram*."

His ﷺ saying, "...and in between them there are ambivalent matters..." i.e. between them there are matters which resemble the *halal* and the *haram* [so that it is not clear what they are]. Where the ambivalence is absent, then disapproval [of that matter] is absent and to ask [further] about it is an innovation. That is [for example] when a stranger comes with goods that he is selling, it is not necessary to make enquiry into it, indeed it is not even desirable, and it is disapproved to ask about it.

His ﷺ saying, "Whoever guards himself against ambivalent matters has secured his *deen* and his honour" i.e. he has sought to have his *deen* free of any blame and safe from any uncertainty. As for the freedom of his honour from blame, if he does not give [the ambivalent matter] up, stupid people would show arrogance towards him by backbiting, and they would attribute to him that he consumed the *haram*, and he would then be a decisive factor in their falling into wrong action. It has been narrated that he ﷺ said, "Whoever believes in Allah and the Last Day let him not take a stance that causes suspicion."[i] There is that 'Ali ؓ said, "Beware of that which hearts reject even if you have an excuse for it, because perhaps you will be unable to make a listener who rejects [your action] listen to [your] excuse." In *Sahih at-Tirmidhi* there is that he ﷺ said, "When any of you breaks wind in the prayer, let him take hold of his nose and then leave." That is so that it would not be said about him, "He broke wind."

His ﷺ saying, "Whoever falls into ambivalent matters will fall into the *haram*" may mean two things, one of which is that he will fall into the *haram* thinking that it is not *haram*. The second is that the meaning would be that he would almost fall into the *haram*, as is said, "Acts of disobedience are the postal service

---

[i] According to 'A'ishah ؓ.

of disbelief" because when a person falls into infringements, he will advance step by step from one corruption to another greater than it. There is an indication of that in His ﷻ words, *"...and* (the Tribe of Isra'il) *killed the Prophets without any right to do so. That was because they disobeyed and went beyond the limits"*[33] meaning that they went step by step from acts of disobedience to killing the prophets. In the hadith there is, "May Allah curse the thief who steals an egg and so his hand is cut off, and who then steals a rope and his [other] hand is cut off"[34] i.e. he will go a step at a time from the egg and the rope [until he is up] to the hilt in theft. The forbidden pasturage (*hima*) is that grass on permitted land which the other person guards. Whoever pastures [his flocks] around a protected pasturage, his cattle will come close to falling within it and thus to pasture in that which the other person has guarded, as opposed to when he pastures his camels far from the protected pasturage.

Know that every forbidden thing has its protected pasturage surrounding it. The private parts are forbidden and the two thighs are their protected pasturage because they are a sanctum (*harim*) for that which is forbidden. Similarly, seclusion with a woman [other than wives, slave-women or family] is the protected zone around that which is forbidden, so that a person must avoid both that which is forbidden and the protected zone around it. That which is forbidden is forbidden for its own sake, and the protected forbidden zone is forbidden because steps are taken by it towards the forbidden.[i]

His ﷺ saying, "Certainly in the body there is a lump of flesh…" i.e. in the body there is a morsel of flesh which, when it has humility then the limbs have humility, and when it is directed then the limbs are directed, and when it is corrupt then the limbs are corrupt. The people of knowledge said that the body

---

[i] In *fiqh* this principle is referred to as *sadd adh-dhara'i*.

is the kingdom of the self and its city. The heart is in the middle of the kingdom. The members are like servants, and the inner faculties are like landed estates of the city. The intellect is like a concerned *wazir* (minister) who advises him (the king). Appetite is a seeker of the servants' provisions. Anger is a policeman and a foul cunning slave who assumes the aspect of a counsellor, but whose advice is deadly poison, and whose untiring habit is always to quarrel with the counselling *wazir*. The faculty of imagination is at the front of the brain like a treasurer, the faculty of thought is in the middle of the brain, and the faculty of memory is in the rear of the brain. The tongue is an interpreter. The five senses are spies. Each one of them has been entrusted with making one of the arts, so the eye has been entrusted with the world of colours, hearing with the world of voices, and so on for all the others, for they are means of information. Then it is said that they are doorkeepers which bring that which they have grasped to the self. It has been said that hearing, sight and the faculty of smell are like capabilities from which the self looks. The heart is the king, so that if the shepherd is sound, the flock will be sound, and if he is corrupt, the flock will be corrupt. His soundness is only obtained by his safety from inner sicknesses such as malice, spite, greed, miserliness, pride, ridicule, showing off, seeking reputation, deceit, covetousness, ambition, and discontent with the decree. There are many illnesses of the heart amounting to almost forty, may Allah heal us of them and make us of those who come to Him with a sound healthy heart.

الحديث السابع

عَنْ أَبِي رُقَيَّةَ تَمِيمِ بْنِ أَوْسٍ الدَّارِيِّ ﷺ أَنَّ النَّبِيَّ ﷺ قَالَ: الدِّينُ النَّصِيحَةُ. قُلْنَا: لِمَنْ؟ قَالَ لِلَّهِ، وَلِكِتَابِهِ، وَلِرَسُولِهِ، وَلِأَئِمَّةِ الْمُسْلِمِينَ وَعَامَّتِهِمْ.

رَوَاهُ مُسْلِمٌ.

7. SINCERITY

Abu Ruqayyah Tamim ibn Aws ad-Dari[i] ﷺ narrated that the Prophet ﷺ said, "The *deen* is sincerity."[ii] We said, "For whom?" He said, "For Allah, His Book, His Messenger, the leaders of the Muslims and their generality." Muslim narrated it.

---

[i] He ﷺ accepted Islam nine years after the *Hijrah*. He was one of the most renowned and best of the companions, and attended battles with the Messenger of Allah ﷺ. He stood at night in prayer with much recitation of Qur'an. He used to complete the recitation of Qur'an in one *rak'ah*, and sometimes he would repeat one *ayah* all night until the morning.

Tamim moved to Sham from Madinah after the murder of 'Uthman ﷺ where he dwelt in Jerusalem and where he died in 40 AH and was buried in Bait Jibril, one of the districts of Khalil (Hebron). Eighteen hadith are narrated from him.

[ii] *An-nasihah* means both sincerity and good advice.

Commentary

[About] his ﷺ saying, "The *deen* is sincerity... for Allah, His Book, His Messenger, the leaders of the Muslims and their generality" al-Khattabi said, "*Nasihah* is a comprehensive word whose meaning is 'the collecting together of a portion of good for the one who is counselled.'" It has been said that *nasihah* is derived from a man's sewing (*nash*) his robe excellently well, so they make a comparison with the action of one who sews, [comparing] that benefit which he [the counsellor] aimed at for the one he advised with [the one who sews] closing up gaps and tears in the robe. It has also been said that it is derived from the clarification (*nash*) of honey when one purifies it of wax, so they made a comparison with the purification of speech from deception with the purification of honey from admixture.

The people of knowledge say that as for sincerity to Allah ﷻ its meaning refers to affirmation of Allah and negation of any partner with Him, abandoning deviations with respect to His attributes, describing Him with all attributes of perfection and majesty, purifying Him, glorious is He and exalted, from every type of shortcoming and defect, undertaking His obedience, avoiding His disobedience, love for His sake and hatred for His sake, affection for whoever obeys Him and enmity for whoever disobeys Him, *jihad* against whoever disbelieves Him, acknowledgement of His blessing and gratitude to Him for it, sincerity in all affairs, calling towards and urging all the above-mentioned qualities, and gentleness with all people or with whomever possible of them. The reality of these qualities returns to the slave in his advising himself, and Allah ﷻ is in no need of the sincerity of those who are sincere.

As for sincerity for the Book of Allah ﷻ it is affirmation that it is the speech of Allah ﷻ and His revelation which nothing of people's speech resembles, and the like of which no one among creation is capable, then honouring it and reciting it as it should be recited, beautifying it, having humility with it, reciting its letters correctly, defending it from the esoteric interpretations of deviants and the opposition of those who refute it, affirmation of what is in it, standing by its rulings, coming to understand its sciences and metaphors, considering its admonitions with respect, reflecting on its wonders, acting on its unambiguous statements and accepting its ambiguous ones, research into its general and specific statements and its abrogating and abrogated [*ayat*], spreading its sciences, inviting others to it and to that which we have mentioned of its good counsel.

As for sincerity to His Messenger ﷺ, it is affirmation of him for the message, affirmation of everything that he brought, obeying him in his command and in his prohibition, helping him in his life and after his death, showing enmity to whoever shows enmity to him and friendship to whoever shows friendship to him, exalting his right and showing respect for him, bringing his way and his Sunnah to life, spreading his *da'wah* and his Sunnah, rejecting any suspicion about it and spreading its sciences and becoming learned in the *fiqh* of it, calling others to it, showing gentleness in learning and teaching it, exalting it and acknowledging its majesty, showing courtesy when reading about it, avoiding talking about it without knowledge, honouring its people because of their relationship to it, taking on its qualities of character and its courtesies, love for the people of his house and his companions, and avoidance of whoever innovates in his Sunnah or shows opposition to anyone of his companions and the like of that.

As for sincerity towards the leaders of the Muslims, it is cooperating with them for the truth and obeying them for it, commanding, forbidding and reminding them with gentleness, informing them of that which they neglect and of the Muslims' rights which have not reached them, not rising against them, and uniting the hearts of the Muslims in obedience to them. Al-Khattabi said, "Part of sincerity towards them is to pray behind them, to wage *jihad* along with them, to pay the *zakah* to them, not to rise against them with the sword if there appear to be injustices or bad behaviour from them, not to persist in false praise of them, and to supplicate for right action for them."[i]

Ibn Battal said, may Allah show him mercy, "In this hadith

---

[i] 'Imam' can be misunderstood as the imam of the prayer which is not the primary meaning intended. Properly the Imam is the Muslim ruler who receives the allegiance of the Muslims living within the Dar al-Islam according to the Sunnah of the Prophet ﷺ and of the *Khulafa'* who took the right way ⁂ and thus it means the *Khalifah*. He either leads the prayers himself or appoints those who lead the prayers.

It must be noted that through much of history there has not been a single undivided Muslim Ummah ruled by one *khalifah*, but sometimes remote lands, such as Andalusia under the historical Murabitun and the Mughal Empire under Aurangzeb, have often pledged allegiance to the *Khalifah* of the time even though it was physically impossible for him to rule and govern their lands directly.

Shehu Uthman dan Fodio of Nigeria, may Allah have mercy on him, took the position that there may be more than one *khalifah* at the same time if their territories are far enough apart that there does not arise a clash between them.

Ibn Juzayy says in *al-Qawanin al-Fiqhiyyah*:

"The pre-conditions of the Imamate (i.e. the caliphate) are eight: Islam, maturity (puberty), intellect (i.e. sanity), maleness, justice, knowledge, competence, and that his descent should be from Quraysh, but on this [last] there is a difference of opinion, so that if people agree [on pledging allegiance] to one who does not meet all of the conditions then it is permitted, from fear of causing dissension and sedition.

"It is not permitted to rise up against the people in authority even if they are tyrannical, unless they openly display clear disbelief. It is obligatory to obey them in whatever a man loves and dislikes, unless they order disobedience [of Allah and His Messenger] for there is no obedience due to a creature if it involves disobedience to the Creator."

there is a proof that sincerity (*nasihah*) is called '*deen*' and 'Islam', and that *deen* signifies action just as it signifies words." He said, "Sincere counsel is an obligation which is fulfilled by whoever undertakes it and therefore is no longer required of the rest." He said, "Sincere counsel is a duty to the extent of one's ability when the one who is counselling knows that his advice will be accepted, his command obeyed and he himself is safe from calamity. If he fears harm then he is at liberty [not to advise or counsel], and Allah ﷻ knows best."

If someone says, "In *Sahih al-Bukhari* there is that he ﷺ said, 'If any of you seeks advice from his brother let him advise him', which indicates that the duty [of giving counsel] is conditional on the request for advice and is not an unqualified [obligation], and that understanding the precondition is a proof that the general statement has a particular meaning", then the answer is that it is possible to understand it in that way with respect to worldly affairs such as marrying a woman or transacting with a man, etc., and the first [hadith] is interpreted to be of a general nature in the affairs of the *deen* which are obligatory duties on every Muslim, and Allah ﷻ knows best.

الحديث الثامن

عَنْ ابنِ عُمَرَ رضِيَ اللَّهُ عَنْهُمَا، أَنَّ رَسُولَ اللَّهِ ﷺ قَالَ: أُمِرْتُ أَنْ أُقَاتِلَ النَّاسَ حَتَّى يَشْهَدُوا أَنْ لَا إِلَهَ إِلَّا اللَّهُ وَأَنَّ مُحَمَّدًا رَسُولُ اللَّهِ، وَيُقِيمُوا الصَّلَاةَ، وَيُؤْتُوا الزَّكَاةَ، فَإِذَا فَعَلُوا ذَلِكَ عَصَمُوا مِنِّي دِمَاءَهُمْ وَأَمْوَالَهُمْ إِلَّا بِحَقِّ الإِسْلَامِ، وَحِسَابُهُمْ عَلَى اللَّهِ تَعَالَى

رَوَاهُ البُخَارِيُّ وَمُسْلِمٌ.

8. Fighting

Ibn 'Umar ؓ narrated that the Messenger of Allah ﷺ said, "I have been commanded to fight people until they witness that there is no god but Allah and that Muhammad is the Messenger of Allah, and they establish the prayer and pay the *zakah*. Then if they do that they are safe from me with respect to their blood and their property except for the right of Islam, and their reckoning is up to Allah, exalted is He." Al-Bukhari and Muslim narrated it.

Commentary

In his ﷺ saying, "I have been commanded..." there is a proof that the unqualified nature of the command and its form mean that it is an obligation [not a recommendation].

If it is said about his ﷺ saying, "Then if they do that they are safe from me with respect to their blood and their property..." that the fast is one of the pillars of Islam and similarly the Hajj, and yet he did not mention them, the answer is that a person is not fought over the fast [if he fails to fast] rather he is imprisoned and denied food and water. As for the Hajj, it has ample time [in which it can be undertaken] so that one is not fought over it. The Messenger of Allah ﷺ only mentioned these three because one is fought for abandoning them, and for this reason he did not mention the fast and the Hajj to Mu'adh when he sent him to the Yemen, rather he reminded him of these three in particular.

As for his ﷺ saying, "...except for the right of Islam...", one of the rights of Islam is the performance of the obligations, and whoever gives up the obligations it is permitted to fight [him], such as rebels, brigands, the assailant, anyone who refuses [to pay] *zakah*, one who refuses to give water to someone in dire need and to domestic animals, criminals, anyone who refuses to pay a debt even though capable of it, the adulterer, and someone who abandons the *jumu'ah* and *wudu'*. In these conditions it is permitted to kill him and to fight him, and similarly if he abandons the [prayer in] congregation. We say that it is an individual obligation or an obligation binding on the community [which if some people perform it the community is freed of any wrong for not having done it].

His ﷺ saying, "...and their reckoning is up to Allah" means that whoever produces the two *shahadahs*, establishes the prayer and produces the *zakah* is protected with respect to his blood and his property. If he has done that with a pure intention he is a believer, and if he has done it dissembling and out of fear of the sword, for example the hypocrite, then his reckoning is up to Allah and He is in charge of the innermost thoughts. Similarly one who performs the prayer without *wudu'* or without having performed *ghusl* after sexual intercourse, or he eats in his house and claims that he is fasting [Ramadan], that is accepted from him and his reckoning is up to Allah, mighty is He and majestic, and Allah knows best.

الحديث التاسع

عَنْ أَبِي هُرَيْرَةَ عَبْدِ الرَّحْمَنِ بْنِ صَخْرٍ ﷺ قَالَ: سَمِعْتُ رَسُولَ اللَّهِ ﷺ يَقُولُ:

مَا نَهَيْتُكُمْ عَنْهُ فَاجْتَنِبُوهُ، وَمَا أَمَرْتُكُمْ بِهِ فَأْتُوا مِنْهُ مَا اسْتَطَعْتُمْ، فَإِنَّمَا أَهْلَكَ الَّذِينَ مِنْ قَبْلِكُمْ كَثْرَةُ مَسَائِلِهِمْ وَاخْتِلَافُهُمْ عَلَى أَنْبِيَائِهِمْ.

رَوَاهُ الْبُخَارِيُّ، وَمُسْلِمٌ.

9. That Which I Forbid You…

Abu Hurairah 'Abd ar-Rahman ibn Sakhr[i] ﷺ said, "I heard the Messenger of Allah ﷺ saying, 'That which I forbid you, avoid it, and that which I command you, do

---

[i] He came to Madinah in 7 AH while the Messenger ﷺ was at Khaibar, and so he went to him, accepted Islam from him and clung to his company devotedly, out of his desire for knowledge. He was the Companion who narrated the most hadith, i.e. 5,374. It is said that 'Umar ﷺ appointed him governor of Bahrain and then later removed him. Later on again he sought to entice him back to the governorship and he refused and repented of the amirate. He lived in Madinah until he died in 57 AH at the end of the khalifate of Mu'awiyah ﷺ when he was seventy-eight years old. He is buried in al-Baqi'.

of it what you are able, for the only thing that destroyed the ones who were before you was their great numbers of questions and their disagreements with their prophets.'" Al-Bukhari and Muslim narrated it.

Commentary

His ﷺ saying, "That which I forbid you, avoid it" that is, avoid it all at once, and do not do it, not even a bit of it. This is of course in the case of a prohibition of something because it is *haram*. As for the prohibition of something in the sense of it being disapproved, then it is permitted to do it. The root of *nahy* (prohibition) linguistically is *man'* 'prevention'.

Concerning his ﷺ saying, "...and that which I command you, do of it that which you are able", there are some issues of which there is, for example, that if one finds water for *wudu'* but it is not sufficient, then the most obvious thing is to use it and then perform *tayammum* for whatever remains [undone]. If one finds only part of a measure (a *sa'*) of grain or other foods for [*zakat*] *al-fitrah* then one must pay that. A consequence of it too is that if one finds only a part of that which suffices for expenditure on a relative, a wife or a domestic animal, it is obligatory to spend it [on them]. This is in contrast [to the case] where one found only a part of a slave [because one had only part ownership] it is not necessary to free him for the expiation of a wrong action, since expiation has an alternative which is fasting.

His ﷺ saying, "...for the only thing that destroyed the ones who were before you was their great numbers of questions and their disagreements with their prophets." Know that there are different degrees of questioning, the first of which is the questioning of an ignorant person about the obligations of the *deen*, such as *wudu'*, prayer, fasting and rulings of ordinary transactions, etc. This type of questioning is obligatory for him according to his saying, "Seeking knowledge is obligatory for every Muslim male and female."³⁵ It is not acceptable for somebody to be silent about that. Allah ﷻ says, *"Ask the People of the Reminder if you do not know."*³⁶ Ibn 'Abbas ﷺ said, "I was given a questioning tongue and an intelligent heart." That was how he himself expressed it about himself ﷺ.

The second division is asking in order to become discerning (*faqih*) in the *deen*, not just for the sake of action alone, for example, for judgements and *fatwas*, and this is a collective obligation because of His ﷻ words, *"If a party from each group of them were to go out so they could increase their knowledge of the deen."*³⁷ He ﷺ said, "Let the one who is present teach the one who is absent."³⁸

The third division is that one asks about something which Allah has not imposed as a duty on one nor on anyone else, and this is the case referred to in this hadith, because there may be in the question a consequent difficulty because of the responsibility which results, and for this reason he ﷺ said, "…and He was silent about some things as a mercy to you, so do not ask about them." It is narrated from 'Ali ﷺ that when *"Hajj to the House is a duty owed to Allah by all mankind – those who can find a way to do it"*³⁹ was revealed, a man said, "Every year, Messenger of Allah?" He ﷺ turned away from him until he repeated the question twice or three times, so the Messenger of Allah ﷺ said, "I am not about to say yes. By Allah, if I said yes, it would become an obligation, and if it became an obligation you would not be able to do it. Leave me alone as long as I leave you alone, for the only thing that destroyed the ones who were before you was their great numbers of questions and their disagreements with their prophets. When I command you to do something, do what you can of it. When I forbid you something, avoid it", and so Allah ﷻ revealed, *"You who believe do not ask about matters which if they were made known* *to you would make things difficult for you*"⁴⁰ i.e. "[which] I have not commanded you to do." This command [in the *ayah*] is particular to his epoch ﷺ. As for after the establishment of the *shari'ah* and security from any increase in it, the prohibition lapsed with the lapse of a reason for it.ⁱ

A group of the first community disapproved of asking about the meanings of ambivalent *ayats*. Malik, may Allah ﷻ show him mercy, [when asked by a man in an assembly] about His ﷻ saying, "*The All-Merciful, established firmly upon the Throne*"⁴¹ said, "The firm establishment is known, its manner is unknown, affirmation of it is obligatory, and asking about it is an innovation, and I see you as an evil man. Eject him from my company." One of them said, "The way of the first community (*salaf*) is safer, and the way of the later communities (*khalaf*) is more learned, and that is questioning."

ⁱ There are no prophets who could now amend it.

الحديث العاشر

عَنْ أَبِي هُرَيْرَةَ ﷺ قَالَ: قَالَ رَسُولُ اللهِ ﷺ:

إِنَّ اللَّهَ طَيِّبٌ لَا يَقْبَلُ إِلَّا طَيِّبًا، وَإِنَّ اللَّهَ أَمَرَ الْمُؤْمِنِينَ بِمَا أَمَرَ بِهِ الْمُرْسَلِينَ فَقَالَ تَعَالَى: يَا أَيُّهَا الرُّسُلُ كُلُوا مِنَ الطَّيِّبَاتِ وَاعْمَلُوا صَالِحًا، وَقَالَ تَعَالَى: يَا أَيُّهَا الَّذِينَ آمَنُوا كُلُوا مِنْ طَيِّبَاتِ مَا رَزَقْنَاكُمْ، ثُمَّ ذَكَرَ الرَّجُلَ يُطِيلُ السَّفَرَ أَشْعَثَ أَغْبَرَ يَمُدُّ يَدَيْهِ إِلَى السَّمَاءِ: يَا رَبِّ يَا رَبِّ وَمَطْعَمُهُ حَرَامٌ، وَمَشْرَبُهُ حَرَامٌ، وَمَلْبَسُهُ حَرَامٌ، وَغُذِّيَ بِالْحَرَامِ، فَأَنَّى يُسْتَجَابُ لَهُ؟

رَوَاهُ مُسْلِمٌ.

10. Pure Wholesome Food

Abu Hurairah said, "The Messenger of Allah said, 'Allah is pure[i] and only accepts that which is pure. Allah ordered the believers with that with which he ordered the Messengers, and He said, "*Messengers, eat of the good things and act rightly*"[42] and He said, "*You who have iman! Eat of the good things We have provided for you,*"'[43] and then he mentioned a dishevelled dusty man lengthening his journey and stretching out his hands to the sky, 'Lord, Lord!' and his food is *haram*, his drink *haram*, his clothing *haram*, he has been fed on the *haram*, so how can he be answered?" Muslim narrated it.

Commentary

About his saying, "Allah is pure (*tayyib*)" it is narrated that 'A'ishah said, "I heard the Messenger of Allah saying, 'O Allah, I ask You by Your blessed, wholesome, pure, purifying name which is most beloved to You, the one which when You are supplicated by it You respond, and when You are asked by it You give, and when You are sought mercy by it You show mercy, and when You are sought to dispel worries by it You dispel worries.'"

The meaning of *tayyib* – 'pure' – is 'free of defects and foul matters', so that it has the meaning of [the Divine name] *al-Quddus* 'The Wholly Pure'. It has been said, "Sweet of praise and the most delicious of the Names to the ones who have gnosis of them." He

---

[i] *Tayyib*, translated as 'good', means literally 'pure, wholesome, sweet, fragrant' and derives from the same root as *'teeb'* which is a perfume, so that *tayyib* has the sense of 'fragrant' a meaning which is reinforced by its opposition in the Qur'an to *khabeeth*, translated variously as 'bad', etc., which means 'foul', 'malodorous' or 'stinking'.

10. Pure Wholesome Food

made His slaves pure to enter the Garden through right actions and made them [the right actions] seem pure and good for them. *Al-kalimah at-tayyibah* – 'the wholesome word' – is "There is no god but Allah."

His ﷺ saying, "...and He only accepts that which is pure" i.e. one cannot draw near to Him by giving something *haram* as *sadaqah* (i.e. *zakah* or voluntary generosity[i]), and it is disliked to give spoiled food as *sadaqah*, such as worm-eaten old grain. Similarly it is disliked to give *sadaqah* of that in which there is some doubt [as to its purity or its status in the *shari'ah*]. Allah ﷻ says, *"Do not have recourse to bad things when you give..."*[44] Just as He ﷻ does not accept [*sadaqah*][ii] from anything but that which is pure, similarly He does not accept any actions but those which are pure and free from the pollution of showing off, conceit, and seeking reputation, etc.

In his ﷺ saying, "He ﷻ said, *'You Messengers, eat of the pure things and do right action'* and He ﷻ said, *'You who believe, eat of the pure things with which We have provided you'"*, what is meant here by 'pure things' is those which are *halal*.[iii] In the hadith there is a proof that a person is rewarded for what he eats if he intends by it to strengthen himself for obedience, or to revive himself – which is one of the duties – as opposed to when he eats purely out of appetite and to enjoy himself.

---

[i] *Sadaqah* is used Qur'anically and in *hadith* and works of *fiqh* for *zakah* as well as for optional acts of giving.

[ii] Thus *zakah* and voluntary *sadaqah* may not be paid with anything which is acquired usuriously, or with a usurious instrument such as a banknote whose origin is as the record of a debt – "I promise to pay the bearer on demand..." since one cannot pay *zakah* with a debt. Paper money's present reality is as fiat money created out of nothing by a small banking elite for the purpose of their own expropriation of the wealth of the planet. It is said that now some three to four hundred families own half of the wealth of the planet.

[iii] It implies too that an essential quality of the *halal* is that it is pure. The word *halal* is often qualified in the Qur'an by the word *tayyib*.

His ﷺ saying, "...and his food is *haram*, his drink *haram*, his clothing *haram*, and he has been fed (*ghudhiya*) on the *haram*" i.e. [*ghudhiya* means that] he has eaten to satiety, and it is with a *dammah* (u) on the *ghayn* with a diacritical point, and a *kasrah* (i) on the *dhal* with a diacritical point, without a *shaddah* (i.e. without a doubling of the *dhal*) from *ghidha* which has *kasrah* (i) [on the *ghayn*] and an *alif maqsurah*. As for *ghadaa'* with a *fathah* (a) [on the *ghayn*] and a *madd* (an extenuation of the second vowel) and a *dal* without a diacritical point, it refers to the same food which is eaten in the early morning (*ghadaa'*).[i] Allah ﷻ says, "*He said to his servant, 'Bring us our morning meal (ghadaa').'*"[45]

His ﷺ saying, "So how can he be answered?" i.e. deeming it unlikely that there should be acceptance or a response to [his] supplication. For this reason al-'Abbadi stipulated that for a supplication to be accepted one must eat *halal* food, but the truth is that that is not a precondition, because He responded to the worst of His creation,[ii] Iblis, and said, "*You are one of the reprieved.*"[46]

---

[i] There can be a certain amount of confusion here, because there are two different Arabic roots, which have slightly different usages classically and in modern times. With the letter *dal*, the word refers to a complex of meanings to do with 'in the morning' and 'tomorrow', and thus gives *ghadaa'* meaning 'early morning' and which is a name of the meal eaten at that time, i.e. 'breakfast', but it is ordinarily used in modern Arabic for the meal eaten after the midday prayer, i.e. 'lunch'. With the letter *dhal*, the word largely refers to nourishment and feeding.

[ii] If Allah answered the supplication of Iblis whom He cursed, then He is free to answer the supplication of a *kafir*, and certainly that of a Muslim who has eaten something *haram*.

الحديث الحادي عشر

عَنْ أَبِي مُحَمَّدٍ الْحَسَنِ بْنِ عَلِيِّ بْنِ أَبِي طَالِبٍ سِبْطِ رَسُولِ اللَّهِ ﷺ وَرَيْحَانَتِهِ رَضِيَ اللَّهُ عَنْهُمَا، قَالَ: حَفِظْتُ مِنْ رَسُولِ اللَّهِ ﷺ

دَعْ مَا يَرِيبُكَ إِلَى مَا لَا يَرِيبُكَ.

رَوَاهُ التِّرْمِذِيُّ، وَالنَّسَائِيُّ، وَقَالَ التِّرْمِذِيُّ: حَدِيثٌ حَسَنٌ صَحِيحٌ.

11. Doubt

Abu Muhammad al-Hasan[i] ibn 'Ali ibn Abi Talib the grandchild of the Messenger of Allah ﷺ and his offspring ﷺ said, "I memorised from the Messenger of Allah ﷺ, 'Abandon that which gives you doubt for that which

---

[i] The son of Fatimah az-Zahra ﷺ he was born in Madinah in 3 AH. He was a year older than his brother al-Husein. He performed the Hajj twenty-five times. Al-Hasan was appointed to the *khilafah* after his father and held it in the Hijaz, Yemen, Iraq and Khurasan for six months. Then his noble and generous character, his forbearance and his caution called him to leave the Khalifate to Mu'awiyah ﷺ out of compassion for the Muslims since they had suffered a great deal from the civil war between 'Ali and Mu'awiyah ﷺ It is important to realise that he is the link between the *Khulafa' ar-Rashidun* ﷺ and the Umayyads to whom he legitimately transferred the *khilafah*.

He died in Madinah in 50 AH. A more substantial biographical outline is to be found in as-Suyuti's *Tarikh al-Khulafa'*, from which the chapters on the *Khulafa' ar-Rashidun* have been translated and published as *The History of the Khalifahs who took the right way*, Ta-Ha Publishers Ltd., London.

gives you no doubt.'" At-Tirmidhi and an-Nasa'i narrated it and at-Tirmidhi said, "A good *sahih* hadith."

Commentary

In his ﷺ saying, "Abandon that which gives you doubt for that which gives you no doubt", there is a proof that the person of *taqwa*[i] ought not to consume[ii] property about which there is some doubt, just as it is forbidden him to consume that which is *haram*.

His ﷺ saying, "...that which gives you no doubt" i.e. turn to that food in which there is no doubt and with which the heart is at ease and about which the self is tranquil. We have already spoken about ambiguity and ambivalence.

---

[i] Ibn Juzayy said, in his dictionary of linguistic meanings of words in Qur'an, "*Taqwa*'s meaning is fear, clinging to obedience to Allah and abandoning disobedience to Him. It is the sum of all good." *Kitab at-tashil li 'ulum at-tanzil.*

[ii] Literally 'eat'. It is appropriate to mention here that the *salaf* were as concerned about eating food bought with *halal* money, as they were about 'halal food' as understood by modern Muslims. They were cautious about accepting the money or eating the food of someone who had acquired his wealth unlawfully, for example the money which derived from the forceful expropriation of an amir or through illegal taxes, or through usury.

A second point that is worth mentioning is that this hadith has a much wider relevance in *fiqh* than just in the domain of food and drink. For example, when a man has a doubt as to whether he has prayed three or four *rak'ahs* for *dhuhr*, then he prays another so that he is certain that he has prayed at least four, and then he performs two extra prostrations after the *salam*. That is another restricted *fiqh* example, and the hadith has a guidance which is vaster than that.

الحديث الثاني عشر

عَنْ أَبِي هُرَيْرَةَ ﷺ قَالَ: قَالَ رَسُولُ اللَّهِ ﷺ

مِنْ حُسْنِ إِسْلَامِ الْمَرْءِ تَرْكُهُ مَا لَا يَعْنِيهِ.

حَدِيثٌ حَسَنٌ، رَوَاهُ التِّرْمِذِيُّ، ابن ماجه هكذا.

12. Leaving What Does Not Concern One

Abu Hurairah said, "The Messenger of Allah said, 'A part of the excellence of a man's Islam is his leaving alone what does not concern him.'" At-Tirmidhi and others relate it like this.

Commentary

His saying, "A part of the excellence of a man's Islam is his leaving alone what does not concern him" i.e. those words and deeds which are of no importance to him of the business of the *deen* and of the world.

He said to Abu Dharr when he asked him about the scrolls of Ibrahim, "They were all proverbs. There was in them, 'Bedazzled ruler! I did not send you to collect possessions one on top of another, but I sent you to avert the supplication of the wronged person from reaching Me, for I do not reject it even if it comes from a disbeliever.' There was in them, 'The intelligent man, as long as his intelligence has not been overcome, must have four hours: an hour in which he holds intimate discourse with his Lord [in prayer and supplication], an hour in which he reflects on the handiwork of Allah ﷻ, an hour in which he speaks with himself [and resolves or makes up his mind], and an hour in which he is in solitary retreat with the Possessor of Majesty and Honour, and that hour will be a help to him for those hours.' In it there was, 'The intelligent man, as long as his intelligence has not been overcome, must not exert himself except for three things: taking provision for the Final Abode, taking some trouble to earn a living, and pleasure in something which is not *haram*.' In it there was, 'The intelligent man, as long as his intelligence has not been overcome, must have insight into his epoch, occupy himself with his affair and guard his tongue, and whoever reckons his speech to be a part of his action will not be about to speak except on what concerns him.'"

I [Abu Dharr] said, "By my father and mother [may you be ransomed], what was there in the scrolls of Musa?" He said, "They were all admonitions. In them there was: 'How astonishing is one who is certain of the Fire, how can he laugh? How astonishing is one who is sure of death, how can he rejoice? How astonishing is one who sees the world and its overturning its people, how can he be at ease in it? How astonishing is one who is certain of the decree and then becomes angry! And how astonishing is one who is sure of the reckoning and does not act!'"

I said, "By my father and mother [may you be ransomed], does anything remain from that which was in their scrolls?" He said, "Yes, Abu Dharr, *'He who has purified himself will have success...'* to the end of the Surah."[i]

I said, "By my father and mother [may you be ransomed],

---

[i] Surat al-A'la: 13-16. "*He who has purified himself will have success, He who invokes the Name of his Lord and prays. Yet still you prefer the life of the dunya when the akhirah is better and longer lasting. This is certainly in the earlier texts, the texts of Ibrahim and Musa.*"

12. Leaving What Does Not Concern One

advise me." He said, "I advise you to have *taqwa* of Allah, for it is the head of all of your affair." He said, "I said, 'Increase me!'" He said, "You must recite the Qur'an (with *tilawah*) and remember Allah a great deal, because He remembers you in Heaven." I said, "Increase me!" He said, "You must wage *jihad* for it is the monasticism of believers." I said, "Increase me!" He said, "You must take to silence because it will repel shaytans from you and it will be a help to you in the matter of your *deen*." I said, "Increase me!" He said, "Say the truth even if it is bitter." I said, "Increase me!" He said, "Do not let blame affect you for the sake of Allah of any who blame." I said, "Increase me!" He said, "Join relationships with your maternal kin even if they sever relationships with you." I said, "Increase me!" He said, "Sufficient evil for a man is that of himself of which he is ignorant, and that which he undertakes which does not concern him. Abu Dharr, there is no intelligence like thoughtful consideration, no caution like restraint and no excellence like excellence of character."[47]

الحديث الثالث عشر

عَنْ أَبِي حَمْزَةَ أَنَسِ بْنِ مَالِكٍ ﷺ خَادِمِ رَسُولِ اللَّهِ ﷺ عَنِ النَّبِيِّ ﷺ قَالَ:

لَا يُؤْمِنُ أَحَدُكُمْ حَتَّى يُحِبَّ لِأَخِيهِ مَا يُحِبُّ لِنَفْسِهِ.

رَوَاهُ الْبُخَارِيُّ، وَمُسْلِمٌ.

13. Loving for One's Brother

Abu Hamzah Anas ibn Malik[i] ﷺ, the servant of the Messenger of Allah ﷺ, narrated that the Prophet ﷺ said, "None of you believes until he loves for his brother what he loves for himself." Al-Bukhari and Muslim narrated it.

---

[i] When the Messenger of Allah ﷺ came to Madinah, Anas' mother came to the Messenger of Allah ﷺ with her son Anas and said to him, "Messenger of Allah take this one as a boy to serve you," and he accepted him. He was then ten years old and he continued to serve him until he ﷺ died and he was at that time well pleased with him.

He went on eight expeditions to battle with the Messenger of Allah ﷺ. He continued to reside in Madinah and witnessed the great conquests of the Companions, being himself present in battle. He used to pray optional prayers and stand in them a great deal. When he concluded a recitation of the Qur'an he would gather his family together and make a supplication for them. Later he resided in Basra where he died in 93 AH, and he was the last of the Companions to die in Basra. 2,286 hadith are narrated from him.

13. *Loving for One's Brother*

Commentary

With respect to his ﷺ saying, "None of you believes until he loves for his brother what he loves for himself", the first thing to be said is that it should be interpreted in terms of the universality of brotherhood[i] even to the extent of encompassing disbelievers and Muslims. One loves for one's disbelieving brother what one loves for oneself: his entrance into Islam, just as one loves for one's Muslim brother his continuance in Islam. For this reason supplication for a disbeliever's guidance is recommended. The hadith proves the incompleteness of the *iman* of whoever does not love for his brother what he loves for himself.

What is meant by 'love' is 'willing good and benefit', moreover what is meant is love in terms of the *deen* and not human love, for human nature may dislike [another's] attainment of good and another's being distinguished over oneself. Man must oppose human nature, supplicate for his brother and wish for him that for which he himself wishes. If a person does not love for his brother what he loves for himself he is envious. Envy, as al-Ghazali said, is in three divisions:

"First, wishing for the removal of another's blessing and one's own attainment of it.

Second, that one wishes for the removal of another's blessing even if one does not oneself gain it, such as when one [already] has the like of it, or one does not even like it [the blessing and want it for oneself], and this is worse than the first.

Third, that one does not wish the removal of another's blessing but one dislikes his elevation above one in good fortune and in rank, and is contented only with equality

---

[i] The Imam is making no equation between the sense of brotherhood here outlined and the Masonic doctrine of the brotherhood of man which achieved its ironic apogee in the French Revolution with the removal of thousands of heads to the accompaniment of the cry *Liberté, Égalité, Fraternité*.

[between oneself and the other] and is not pleased with any extra [the other might have over one], and this too is forbidden because one is not contented with the apportioning of Allah, exalted is He. Allah ﷻ says, '*Is it, then, they who allocate the mercy of your Lord? We have allocated...*'[i] Whoever is not pleased with the allocation [of blessings which Allah ﷻ has made] opposes Allah ﷻ in His apportioning and His wisdom. Man must master his self and bring it to contentment with the Decree, and oppose it by making supplication for his enemy in a way which opposes the self."

---

[i] Surat az-Zukhruf: 32. "*Is it, then, they who allocate the mercy of your Lord? We have allocated their livelihood among them in the life of the dunya and raised some of them above others in rank so that some of them are subservient to others.*" This is a clear refutation of those who declare that Islam requires equality between people, a doctrine deriving from the French Revolution's '*Égalité*'.

الحديث الرابع عشر

عَنْ ابْنِ مَسْعُودٍ ﷺ قَالَ: قَالَ رَسُولُ اللهِ ﷺ

لَا يَحِلُّ دَمُ امْرِئٍ مُسْلِمٍ إِلَّا بِإِحْدَى ثَلَاثٍ: الثَّيِّبُ الزَّانِي، وَالنَّفْسُ بِالنَّفْسِ، وَالتَّارِكُ لِدِينِهِ الْمُفَارِقُ لِلْجَمَاعَةِ.

رَوَاهُ الْبُخَارِيُّ، ومُسْلِمٌ.

14. The Sanctity of a Muslim's Blood

Ibn Mas'ud ؓ said, "The Messenger of Allah ﷺ said, 'The blood of a Muslim man is not permitted [to be shed] except for one of three: the adulterous mature person [who is or has been married], a person [killed in retaliation] for [the killing of] a person, and one who abandons his *deen* and separates himself from the community." Al-Bukhari and Muslim narrated it.

Commentary

By his ﷺ saying, "...*ath-thayyib az-zani* – the adulterous mature person", is meant someone who marries, has intercourse in a valid marriage and then commits adultery after that, for he is to be stoned, even if he is not married at the time of the adultery, because of his having the attribute of being *muhsan* (i.e. having married and consummated a marriage).

His ﷺ saying, "...a person [killed in retaliation] for [killing] a person" i.e. [homicide] with the precondition of equality, for a Muslim is not killed for [killing] a disbeliever, nor a free man for [killing] a slave according to the Shafi'is but not the Hanafis.

His ﷺ saying, "...and someone who abandons his *deen* and separates himself from the community", who is a renegade and refuge is sought with Allah [from such a thing happening]. He may attach himself to a community, like a Jew who becomes a Christian and vice-versa; he is not killed because he has abandoned his *deen* although he has not separated himself from the community. On this there are two sayings the most sound of which is that he is not killed, on the contrary he is classed as a believer. The second view is that he is killed because he has come to believe in the falsity of the *deen* in which he used to be and has changed to a *deen* which he used to think false before that, and that is untrue so he is not left alone, indeed if he does not accept Islam he is killed,[i] and the

---

[i] In the *Muwatta'* of Imam Malik ibn Anas, may Allah show him mercy, on this issue there is: "Yahya narrated to us from Malik from Zayd ibn Aslam that the Messenger of Allah ﷺ said, 'Whoever changes his *deen*, then strike his neck.'"

This is a *mursal* hadith since Zayd ibn Aslam was not a Companion. However, al-Bukhari narrated the same meaning from Ayyub from 'Ikrimah from Ibn 'Abbas as, "Whoever alters his *deen*, then kill him."

Malik says about it: "The meaning of the saying of the Prophet ﷺ as we see it and Allah knows best, 'Whoever changes his *deen*, then strike his neck' is that whoever goes out of Islam to something other than it such as heretics, etc., then if those are learnt of they are killed without being sought to repent because their repentance is not recognised, and because they used to conceal their disbelief and make their Islam public. I do not think that those should be sought to repent, and their word is not accepted. As for whoever leaves Islam for some other [religion] and makes that public, then

14. The Sanctity of a Muslim's Blood

killing proceeds in a form which has already been discussed.[i]

---

he is asked to repent and if he does [it is accepted], and if not he is killed. That is because if people are on that they are invited to Islam and asked to repent [of their disbelief], and if they repent that is accepted from them, and if they do not repent they are killed. He did not mean by it, in our opinion, and Allah knows best, whoever leaves Judaism for Christianity, nor one who leaves Christianity for Judaism, nor anyone of any of the religions who changes his religion, except for Islam. Whoever leaves Islam for something else and makes that public, that is the one who is meant by it, and Allah knows best."

[i] This judgment can only take place after the person concerned has been reasoned with and given an opportunity to change his mind, and, moreover, only in a polity in which the *deen* has been put into effect. As with other legal judgments, they cannot be discharged outside of such a situation.

الحديث الخامس عشر

عَنْ أَبِي هُرَيْرَةَ ﷺ أَنَّ رَسُولَ اللهِ ﷺ قَالَ:

مَنْ كَانَ يُؤْمِنُ بِاللهِ وَالْيَوْمِ الْآخِرِ فَلْيَقُلْ خَيْرًا أَوْ لِيَصْمُتْ، وَمَنْ كَانَ يُؤْمِنُ بِاللهِ وَالْيَوْمِ الْآخِرِ فَلْيُكْرِمْ جَارَهُ، وَمَنْ كَانَ يُؤْمِنُ بِاللهِ وَالْيَوْمِ الْآخِرِ فَلْيُكْرِمْ ضَيْفَهُ.

رَوَاهُ الْبُخَارِيُّ، وَمُسْلِمٌ.

15. WHOEVER BELIEVES IN ALLAH AND THE LAST DAY

Abu Hurairah narrated that the Messenger of Allah said, "Whoever believes in Allah and the Last Day then let him speak well or remain silent. Whoever believes in Allah and the Last Day then let him generously honour[i] his neighbour. Whoever believes in Allah and the Last Day then

---

[i] Note that the Arabic root signifies both nobility and generosity, so the hadith could also be translated: "…let him honour, treat nobly, or be generous to…"

let him generously honour his guest." Al-Bukhari and Muslim narrated it.

Commentary

About his ﷺ saying, "Whoever believes in Allah and the Last Day then let him speak well or remain silent", ash-Shafi'i said, may Allah show him mercy, "The meaning of the hadith is that when one intends to speak one should reflect and if it appears that there is no harm in talking, then one should talk. If it appears that there is harm in it or there is doubt in it, then one should remain silent."

The magnificent Imam Abu Muhammad ibn Abi Zayd [al-Qayrawani], the Imam of the Malikis in the Maghrib in his time, said, "All the courtesies of good branch off from four hadith: the saying of the Prophet ﷺ, 'Whoever believes in Allah and the Last Day then let him speak well or remain silent,' and his ﷺ saying, 'A part of the excellence of a man's Islam is his abandoning that which does not concern him,' and his ﷺ saying to the one who asked him to give him concise and summary advice, 'Do not become angry!' and his saying, 'None of you believes until he loves for his brother what he loves for himself.'"

It has been transmitted that Abu'l-Qasim al-Qushayri said, may Allah show him mercy, "Silence at its time is a quality of men, just as speaking at the right place is one of the noblest of qualities." He said, "I heard Abu 'Ali ad-Daqqaq saying, 'Whoever withholds himself from speaking the truth is a dumb shaytan,' and he narrated it similarly in *Hilyat al-'Ulama* (The States of the Men of Knowledge) from more than one person. In *Hilyat al-Awliya* (The States of the Close Friends [of Allah]) there is that man ought not to let any speech issue from him except that which he needs, just as he does not spend of his earnings except that which he needs." He said, "If you were to purchase paper for the recording angels you would withhold a great deal of speech."

It is narrated from him ﷺ that he said, "Part of a man's *fiqh* is his speaking little about what does not concern him." It is narrated from him ﷺ that he said, "Well-being has ten portions, nine of which consist of silence except in remembrance of Allah, mighty is He and majestic."

It is said, "Whoever is silent and so is safe, is as whoever speaks and gains."

It was said to someone, "Why do you cling to silence?" He said, "Because I have never ever regretted silence, but I continually regret speech."

One thing which is said is, "The wound [caused] by the tongue is like the wound [caused] by the hand."

It has been said, "The tongue is a beast of prey, if it is left alone it savages."

It is narrated from 'Ali ؓ:

"The youth dies from the slip of his tongue,
 but the man does not die from the slip of his foot,
for the slip of his mouth shoots at his head
 but the slip of his foot [only] slows him up."

One thing that has been said is:

"The silent dumb person is successful,
 his speech is reckoned as nourishment.
Not every speech has an answer,
 an answer that the silent one will disapprove.
And how astonishing is a wrongdoing man
 who is sure that he will die."

About his ﷺ saying, "Whoever believes in Allah and the Last Day then let him generously honour his neighbour, and whoever believes in Allah and the Last Day then let him generously honour his guest", Qadi 'Iyad said, "The meaning of the hadith is that whoever adheres to the laws of Islam holds fast to honouring guests and neighbours generously." He ﷺ said, "Jibril continued advising me about the neighbour so much that I thought he would make him inherit."⁴⁸ He ﷺ said, "Whoever harms his neighbour then Allah will give him possession of his house." [There is also] His ﷻ saying, *"...and to neighbours who are related to you and neighbours who are not related to you."*ⁱ

The term 'neighbour' pertains to four: [first] those who inhabit your house with you. The poet said:

"O our neighbour in the house,
   You are divorced."

It also refers to whoever adjoins your house, it refers to forty houses on every side, and it refers to whoever resides with you in the same land. Allah ﷻ says, *"Then they will only be your neighbours there a very short time."*⁴⁹ An immediate Muslim neighbour who is a relative has three rights,ⁱⁱ an unrelated Muslim neighbour has two rights,ⁱⁱⁱ and an unrelated non-Muslim has one right.ⁱᵛ

Hospitality is a part of the courtesy of Islam, one of the characteristics of the prophets and people of right action. Al-Layth considered [extending hospitality for] one night an obligation. However, they disagree as to whether hospitality is an obligation on [both] a city dweller and on a country person or whether it is especially an obligation on a country dweller. Malik and Sahnun held that it is an obligation on country dwellers because travellers can find hotels and places to stay in the city, and they can buy what they need in the markets. It has been narrated in the hadith literature, "Hospitality is [an obligation] on the people

---

ⁱ Surat an-Nisā': 36. *"...wa'l-jari dhi'l-qurba wa'l-jari'l-junubi..."* "Ibn 'Abbas said, *'wa'l-jari dhi'l-qurba* is the near relative and *al-jari'l-junubi* is the non-relative.' It has also been said that *dhi'l-qurba* is the one who lives near to you and *al-junubi* is the one who lives far away from you. According to some of them the limit at which a neighbourhood ends is forty cubits on every side." Ibn Juzayy from the *tafsir* of the above *ayah* in *Kitab at-tashil li 'ulum at-tanzil*.

ⁱⁱ Because of his Islam, his kinship and his being a neighbour.

ⁱⁱⁱ Because of his Islam and his being a neighbour.

ⁱᵛ Because of his being a neighbour.

of deserts [tent dwellers] and it is not [an obligation] on city dwellers", however this is a fabricated hadith.

الحديث السادس عشر

عَنْ أَبِي هُرَيْرَةَ ﷺ أَنَّ رَجُلًا قَالَ لِلنَّبِيِّ ﷺ أَوْصِنِي. قَالَ: لَا تَغْضَبْ، فَرَدَّدَ مِرَارًا، قَالَ: لَا تَغْضَبْ.

رَوَاهُ الْبُخَارِيُّ.

16. Do Not Become Angry

Abu Hurairah ❁ narrated that, "A man said to the Prophet ❁, 'Advise me.' He said, 'Do not become angry' and repeated it several times, saying, 'Do not become angry.'" Al-Bukhari and Muslim narrated it.

Commentary

The meaning of his ❁ saying, "Do not become angry" is do not carry out or execute your anger, and the prohibition does not refer to anger itself, because it is a part of human nature which man is not able to repel.

He ❁ said, "Beware of anger because it is a burning coal kindled in the heart of the son of Adam. Do you not see how when one of you becomes angry, his eyes become red and his external jugular veins become swollen. When any of you senses something of that then let him lie down on his bed or on the ground."[50]

A man came to the Prophet ❁ and said, "Messenger of Allah teach me something which will draw me near to the Garden and keep me far from the Fire." He said, "Do not become angry and the Garden is yours."[51]

He ﷺ said, "Anger is from shaytan and shaytan is created from fire; the only thing which puts out fire is water so when any of you becomes angry let him perform *wudu'*."[52]

Abu Dharr al-Ghifari said, "The Messenger of Allah ﷺ said to us, 'When any of you becomes angry while he is standing let him sit down. Then if the anger leaves him [well and good], and if not let him lie down.'"[53]

'Isa ﷺ said to Yahya ibn Zakariyya ﷺ, "I will teach you some useful knowledge: do not become angry." He said, "How can I not become angry?" He said, "If someone mentions to you something [a defect or wrong] that is within you then say, 'A wrong which you have mentioned and for which I seek forgiveness of Allah.' If someone mentions to you something [a defect or wrong] which is not in you, then praise Allah since He did not put that with which you are reproached in you, and it is a good deed which is meant for you."

'Amr ibn al-'As ﷺ said, "I asked the Messenger of Allah ﷺ about that which would keep me far from the anger of Allah ﷺ and he said, 'Do not become angry.'"

Luqman said to his son, "If you want to take someone as a brother, then make him angry, and if he is fair to you while he is angry [then take him as a brother] and if not then beware of him."

$$\text{الحديث السابع عشر}$$

عَنْ أَبِي يَعْلَى شَدَّادِ بْنِ أَوْسٍ ﷺ عَنْ رَسُولِ اللَّهِ ﷺ قَالَ: إِنَّ اللَّهَ كَتَبَ الْإِحْسَانَ عَلَى كُلِّ شَيْءٍ، فَإِذَا قَتَلْتُمْ فَأَحْسِنُوا الْقِتْلَةَ، وَإِذَا ذَبَحْتُمْ فَأَحْسِنُوا الذِّبْحَةَ، وَلْيُحِدَّ أَحَدُكُمْ شَفْرَتَهُ، وَلْيُرِحْ ذَبِيحَتَهُ.

رَوَاهُ مُسْلِمٌ.

17. Allah has Decreed Excellence for Everything

Abu Ya'la Shaddad ibn Aws[i] ﷺ narrated that the Messenger of Allah ﷺ said, "Allah has decreed excellence (*ihsan*[ii]) for everything, so when you kill, do the killing excellently

---

[i] He used to unite wisdom and knowledge. When he went to bed he would toss and turn, and sleep would not come to him, so he would say, "O Allah, the Fire has made me sleepless and has driven sleep far away from me." Then he would stand and pray until morning. Shaddad resided at al-Bayt al-Maqdis; he was born there and died there in 58 AH at seventy-five years of age. Fifty hadith are narrated from him.

[ii] We have already seen *ihsan* in hadith number 2 on Islam, *iman* and *ihsan*. *Ihsan* is from the same root as '*hasan*' which means both 'good' and 'beautiful', and *ihsan* has the sense of making an act good and beautiful. It is a degree which is superior to right action because it is not only right but beautiful.

well, and when you slaughter [an animal], perform the slaughter excellently well, and let any of you sharpen his knife and let him put the animal at ease." Muslim narrated it.

Commentary

[With respect to] his ﷺ saying, "Allah has decreed excellence for everything", a part of the whole quality of *ihsan* (excellence) in the killing of a Muslim in retaliation [for murder] is that one should acquaint oneself with the instrument of retaliation and not kill with a worn-out old instrument. Similarly, one should sharpen the knife at the time of slaughtering [an animal] and give the beast some ease. Nor should one cut anything from it until it is dead, nor sharpen the knife in front of it, and one should offer it water before slaughter. One should not slaughter a milking animal nor one which has a young one until it has no need of the milk. One should not be rough while milking and one should trim one's nails at milking. They say, "One [animal] should not be slaughtered in front of the other."[i]

---

[i] It is important to note here that the modern industrial process, driven by the insane greed and anxiety which motivates usury, does not honour any of the above courtesies of slaughter sometimes even when it is so-called '*halal*' meat.

الحديث الثامن عشر

عَنْ أَبِي ذَرٍّ جُنْدُبِ بْنِ جُنَادَةَ، وَأَبِي عَبْدِ الرَّحْمَنِ مُعَاذِ بْنِ جَبَلٍ رَضِيَ اللَّهُ عَنْهُمَا، عَنْ رَسُولِ اللَّهِ ﷺ قَالَ: اتَّقِ اللَّهَ حَيْثُمَا كُنْتَ، وَأَتْبِعِ السَّيِّئَةَ الْحَسَنَةَ تَمْحُهَا، وَخَالِقِ النَّاسَ بِخُلُقٍ حَسَنٍ.

رَوَاهُ التِّرْمِذِيُّ وَقَالَ: حَدِيثٌ حَسَنٌ، وَفِي بَعْضِ النُّسَخِ: حَسَنٌ صَحِيحٌ.

18. Have Taqwa of Allah Wherever you are

Abu Dharr Jundub ibn Junadah[i] and Abu 'Abd ar-Rahman Mu'adh ibn Jabal ⬥ narrated that the Messenger of Allah ﷺ said, "Have *taqwa* of Allah wherever you are

---

[i] He was from the tribe of Ghifar who lived in the desert and he came to Makkah because he had heard a rumour of the sending of the Prophet ﷺ. When he met him, he was one of the very first to accept Islam. Then he returned to his tribe and stayed with them until the *Hijrah*, and his brother Anees and a half of the tribe accepted Islam from him. When the Prophet ﷺ came to Madinah the other half of the tribe accepted Islam. He was one of the most abstinent of men with a great capacity for knowledge. The Chosen

and follow up a wrong action with a good action which will efface it, and treat people good-naturedly." At-Tirmidhi narrated it, and said, "A good hadith," and in some copies, "Good, *sahih.*"

Commentary

His ﷺ saying, "Have *taqwa* of Allah wherever you are" i.e. have *taqwa* of Him in solitude as you have *taqwa* of Him in the presence of people, and have *taqwa* of Him in all other places and at all other times. Something that is an aid to *taqwa* is to become conscious that Allah ﷻ is watchful over the slave in all of his states. Allah ﷻ says, *"Three men cannot confer together secretly without Him being the fourth of them."*[54]

Taqwa is a comprehensive word comprising the performance of the obligations and the giving up of what is forbidden.[i]

His ﷺ saying, "...and follow up a wrong action with a good which will efface it" i.e. when you have done a wrong action seek forgiveness of Allah for it and after it do a good action to efface it.

Know that the apparent meaning of this hadith seems to indicate that a good action only effaces one wrong action even though each good action is worth ten, but that multiples [of rewards for a good action] do not efface a wrong action, but this is not the apparent meaning. Rather one good action effaces ten wrong actions, and in the hadith literature there is evidence of that, which is his ﷺ saying, "Declare Allah to be greater [with *Allahu akbar*] after each prayer ten times, and praise [Him with *al-hamdulillah*] ten times and glorify [Him with *subhan'Allah*] ten

---

One ﷺ bore witness that he was one of the most truthful men. He lived at the end of his life in ar-Rabdhah some distance from Madinah towards Iraq where he died in 31 AH. 281 hadith are narrated from him.

[i] *Taqwa* does contain an element of fear of Allah.

18. Have Taqwa of Allah Wherever you are

times. That is one hundred and fifty[i] on the tongue, and one thousand five hundred in the scales." Then he ﷺ said, "Which of you can do one thousand five hundred bad deeds in one day?"[55] indicating that multiple [rewards for a single right action] do efface wrong actions.

The apparent meaning of the hadith is that a good action effaces wrong actions unqualifiedly, however it has to be interpreted as wrong actions connected to a right due to Allah, exalted is He. As for wrong actions connected to rights due to slaves [of Allah] such as anger, backbiting and telling tales, nothing effaces them except the slave [whom one has wronged] considering it undone (i.e. they must forgive it), and one must specify to him the nature of the wrongdoing, saying, "I said such and such against you."

In the hadith there is an indication that taking oneself to account is an obligation. He ﷺ said, "Take yourselves to account before you are taken to account." Allah ﷻ says, *"You who have iman! Have taqwa of Allah and let each self look to what it has sent forward for Tomorrow."*[56]

[About] his ﷺ saying, "...and treat people good-naturedly", know that good nature (*al-khuluq al-hasan*) is a comprehensive phrase for showing excellent behaviour to people and withholding harm from them. He ﷺ said, "You cannot encompass people with your property, so encompass them with an open face and good nature."[57] From him ﷺ there is, "The best of you is the best of you in character."[58] From him ﷺ there is that a man came to him and said, "Messenger of Allah, what is the best action?" He said, "Good nature"[59] and it is based on what we had previously of, "Do not become angry."

It is said that a prophet complained to his Lord about his wife's bad nature and Allah ﷻ revealed to him, "I have made that your portion of harm." Abu Hurairah ﷺ said, "The Messenger of Allah

---

[i] With five prayers a day.

ﷺ said, 'The most perfect of believers in belief is the best of them in character, and the best of them are those who are best towards their women.'"⁶⁰ From him ﷺ there is that he said, "Allah has chosen Islam for you as a *deen*, so honour it with good nature and liberal generosity, because it is incomplete without them."⁶¹ Jibril عليه السلام said to the Prophet ﷺ when *"Make allowances (al-'afw) for people"*ⁱ was revealed, he said in explanation of it, "That you pardon whoever wrongs you, and keep up relations with someone who severs relations with you, and give to someone who withholds from you." Allah ﷻ says, *"Repel the bad with something better..."*ⁱⁱ

It was said in explanation of the *ayah*, *"Indeed you are truly vast in character"*⁶² that "His nature was the Qur'an, he was bound by its command, checked by its reproof, contented with that with which it was contented and displeased with that with which it was displeased, may Allah bless him and grant him peace."

---

[i] Surat al-A'raf: 199. *'Afw* is literally 'pardoning' which is to forget even that the wrong was done one.
[ii] Surah Fussilat: 34. *"Repel the bad with something better and, if there is enmity between you and someone else, he will be like a bosom friend."*

الحديث التاسع عشر

عَنْ عَبْدِ اللَّهِ بْنِ عَبَّاسٍ رضيَ اللَّهُ عَنْهُمَا قَالَ: كُنْتُ خَلْفَ رَسُولِ اللَّهِ ﷺ يَوْمًا، فَقَالَ: يَا غُلَامُ! إِنِّي أُعَلِّمُكَ كَلِمَاتٍ: احْفَظِ اللَّهَ يَحْفَظْكَ، احْفَظِ اللَّهَ تَجِدْهُ تُجَاهَكَ، إِذَا سَأَلْتَ فَاسْأَلِ اللَّهَ، وَإِذَا اسْتَعَنْتَ فَاسْتَعِنْ بِاللَّهِ، وَاعْلَمْ أَنَّ الأُمَّةَ لَوِ اجْتَمَعَتْ عَلَى أَنْ يَنْفَعُوكَ بِشَيْءٍ لَمْ يَنْفَعُوكَ إِلَّا بِشَيْءٍ قَدْ كَتَبَهُ اللَّهُ لَكَ، وَإِنِ اجْتَمَعُوا عَلَى أَنْ يَضُرُّوكَ بِشَيْءٍ لَمْ يَضُرُّوكَ إِلَّا بِشَيْءٍ قَدْ كَتَبَهُ اللَّهُ عَلَيْكَ، رُفِعَتِ الأَقْلَامُ، وَجَفَّتِ الصُّحُفُ.

رَوَاهُ التِّرْمِذِيُّ وَقَالَ: حَدِيثٌ حَسَنٌ صَحِيحٌ. وَفِي رِوَايَةِ غَيْرِ التِّرْمِذِيِّ:

اِحْفَظِ اللَّهَ تَجِدْهُ أَمَامَكَ، تَعَرَّفْ إِلَى اللَّهِ فِي الرَّخَاءِ يَعْرِفْكَ فِي الشِّدَّةِ، وَاعْلَمْ أَنَّ مَا أَخْطَأَكَ لَمْ يَكُنْ لِيُصِيبَكَ، وَمَا أَصَابَكَ لَمْ يَكُنْ لِيُخْطِئَكَ، وَاعْلَمْ أَنَّ النَّصْرَ مَعَ الصَّبْرِ، وَأَنَّ الْفَرَجَ مَعَ الْكَرْبِ، وَأَنَّ مَعَ الْعُسْرِ يُسْرًا.

19. BE MINDFUL OF ALLAH, AND HE WILL BE MINDFUL OF YOU

Abu'l-'Abbas 'Abdullah ibn 'Abbas[i] said, "I was behind the Prophet [on a camel] one day, and he said to me, 'Boy, I will teach you some words: Be mindful of Allah and He will be mindful of you. Be mindful of Allah and you will find Him in front of you. When you ask then ask Allah. When you seek help then seek help from Allah. Know that if the Ummah gathered together to benefit you with something, they would not benefit you except with something that Allah had already written for you. If

---

[i] He was born three years before the *Hijrah*. He was named *"Tarjuman al-Qur'an* – The Translator of the Qur'an", and was known as "The Ocean" because of the vastness of his knowledge. In a hadith with an authentic *isnad*, the Prophet supplicated for him saying, "O Allah give him discernment in the *deen* and teach him the inner meaning." 1,660 hadith are narrated from him. He died in Ta'if in 68 AH when he was seventy-one years old. Muhammad ibn al-Hanafiyyah, a son of 'Ali through a later wife al-Hanafiyyah, led the funeral prayer for him, and he said, "There has died, by Allah, this day the best of this Ummah."

they gathered together to harm you with something, they would not harm you except with something that Allah had already written against you. The pens have been lifted and the pages are dry." At-Tirmidhi related it and said, "A good *sahih* hadith."

In a narration apart from that of at-Tirmidhi there is, "Be mindful of Allah and you will find Him in front of you. Make yourself known to Allah in ample circumstances, He will acknowledge you [when you are] in severe difficulty. Know that what has missed you was never going to befall you and what has befallen you was never going to miss you. Know that help is with patience, deliverance is with distress, and that with difficulty there is ease."

Commentary

His ﷺ saying, "Be mindful of Allah and He will be mindful of you" means be mindful of His commands and follow them, and keep within His prohibitions, He will be mindful of you in your ups and downs, in your world and in your next life. Allah ﷻ says, *"Anyone who acts rightly, male or female, being a mu'min, We will give them a good life."*[63] Whatever trials and afflictions come to a slave are because of his neglect of the commands of Allah. Allah ﷻ says, *"Any disaster that strikes you is through what your own hands have earned."*[64]

[About] his ﷺ saying, "You will find Him in front of you", he ﷺ said, "Make yourself known to Allah in ample circumstances, He will acknowledge you [when you are] in severe difficulty." Allah ﷻ clearly states in His book that right action benefits one in difficult circumstances and rescues one who does it, and that wrong action leads to severe difficulty. Allah ﷻ says in telling the story of Yunus ﷺ, *"Had it not been that he was a man who glorified*

Allah, he would have remained inside its belly until the Day they are raised again."⁶⁵ When Fir'awn said, *"I believe that there is no god but Him in whom the tribe of Israel believe"* then the angel said to him, *"What, now! When previously you rebelled and were one of the corrupters?"*⁶⁶

His ﷺ saying, "When you ask, then ask Allah" indicates that a slave ought not to connect his secret to other than Allah, rather he should trust in Him in all of his affairs. Moreover, if the need for which he is asking is one of those which is not customarily found in the hands of people such as seeking guidance, knowledge, understanding of the Qur'an and Sunnah, the healing of sickness, and attainment of safety from the trials of the world and from the torment of the next life, then he must ask his Lord for that. If the necessity for which he is asking is one which customarily Allah, glorious is He and exalted, places in the hands of His creation, such as necessities connected to craftsmen, manufacturers and people in governance, then he should ask Allah ﷻ to make their hearts kind towards him, saying, "O Allah make the hearts of Your male and female slaves kind towards me," etc. He must not ask Allah to grant him independence from people, because he ﷺ heard 'Ali saying, "O Allah give us independence from Your creation" and he said to him, "Do not say this, for some of the creation need others,ⁱ but rather say:

$$\text{اَللّٰهُمَّ أَغْنِنَا عَنْ شِرَارِ خَلْقِكَ}$$

'O Allah give us independence from the corrupt ones of Your creation.'" As for asking people and depending on them, that is blameworthy. It is related from Allah ﷻ in the revealed books, "Does he knock with [his] thoughts on the door of someone other than Me while My door is open? He wishes, and is anyone wished for in distressing circumstances other than Me, and I am

---

ⁱ The creation is interdependent.

19. Be Mindful of Allah, and He will be Mindful of you

the Powerful King? I will dress whoever wishes for other than Me in a robe of humiliation among people..."

His ﷺ saying, "And know that if the Ummah...", since man hopes for good treatment from whomever he loves, and fears bad treatment from whomever he is wary of, Allah asserts the hopelessness of [expecting] any benefit from people by His saying, *"If Allah afflicts you with harm, no one can remove it except Him. If He desires good for you, no one can avert His favour."*[67] Nor does any of this negate His ﷺ saying when He relates the story of Musa ﷺ, *"and I am afraid they will kill me"*[68] and His ﷺ saying, *"...we are afraid that he might persecute us or overstep the bounds"*[69] and similarly His saying, *"Take all necessary precautions"*[70] etc. Indeed safety is by the decree of Allah and destruction is by the decree of Allah, and man flees from the causes of destruction to the causes of safety. Allah ﷺ says, *"Do not cast yourselves into destruction."*[71] There is his ﷺ saying, *"Know that help is with patience"* and he ﷺ said, "Do not wish to meet the enemy, and ask Allah for safety. If you meet them be patient and do not run away, for truly Allah is with those who are patient." Similarly, patience in affliction in a place is followed by help, for there is his ﷺ saying, "Truly deliverance is with distress *(karb)*" and distress is 'a severe trial', so when the trial is severe, Allah ﷺ follows it with deliverance, as it is said, "Crisis, be severe! You will pass."

His ﷺ saying, *"Truly with difficulty there is ease"*[i] and it has been narrated in another hadith that he said, "A difficulty will never overcome two eases" and that is that Allah mentioned difficulty twice and He mentioned ease twice, but according to the Arabs whenever a definite noun is repeated it is singular since the second definite article is for distinguishing a noun as

---

[i] 'Abdullah Ibrahim al-Ansari says that this is a hadith which is agreed upon. There is also the word of Allah ﷺ, *"For truly with hardship comes ease; truly with hardship comes ease."* Surat al-Inshirah: 5-6.

one already known to the reader and hearer [and thus there is only one difficulty mentioned but two eases].[i]

---

[i] Some of the people of knowledge have pointed out that Allah ﷻ says, *"Allah will appoint after difficulty, ease"* Surat at-Talaq: 7, and that this is the second ease mentioned in the Qur'an which comes after the difficulty, as well as the ease which is with the difficulty, and Allah knows best.

الحديث العشرون

عَنْ أَبِي مَسْعُودٍ عُقْبَةَ بْنِ عَمْرٍو الْأَنْصَارِيِّ الْبَدْرِيِّ ﷺ قَالَ: قَالَ رَسُولُ اللَّهِ ﷺ:

إِنَّ مِمَّا أَدْرَكَ النَّاسُ مِنْ كَلَامِ النُّبُوَّةِ الْأُولَى: إِذَا لَمْ تَسْتَحِ فَاصْنَعْ مَا شِئْتَ.

رَوَاهُ الْبُخَارِيُّ.

20. Shame and Modesty

Abu Mas'ud 'Uqbah ibn 'Amr al-Ansari al-Badri[i] ﷺ said, "The Messenger of Allah ﷺ said, 'A part of that which people understood from the speech of the first prophethood is: If you have no shame, do what you want.'" Al-Bukhari narrated it.

Commentary

His ﷺ saying, "If you have no shame, do what you want" means that when you want to do something, if it is something of which

---

[i] He was not present at Badr, but he was called Badri because he resided there. He later lived in Kufa and built a home there. He died in Madinah in 41 AH. 102 hadith are narrated from him.

you are not ashamed before Allah – not before people – of doing, then do it, and if not then do not do it. All of Islam pivots around this hadith, and based on this [understanding] is his ﷺ saying, "Do what you want." There are those who interpret the hadith in the sense that if you are not ashamed before Allah ﷻ and are not fearfully watchful of Allah then give your self its desire and do what it wants; so that then the command in it is for the purpose of threatening in order to frighten, not in the sense of declaring it permissible, and it would be as His ﷻ saying, *"Do what you like..."*[i] and like His ﷻ saying, *"Stir up any of them you can with your voice."*[ii]

---

[i] *"Do what you like. He sees whatever you do."* Surah Fussilat: 40. The command to do whatever one wants is coupled with the reminder of Allah's seeing one's actions.

[ii] Surat al-Isra': 64. The *ayah* is addressed to Iblis.

الحديث الحادي والعشرون

عَنْ أَبِي عَمْرٍو وَقِيلَ: أَبِي عَمْرَةَ سُفْيَانَ بْنِ عَبْدِ اللَّهِ ﷺ قَالَ: قُلْتُ: يَا رَسُولَ اللَّهِ قُلْ لِي فِي الْإِسْلَامِ قَوْلًا لَا أَسْأَلُ عَنْهُ أَحَدًا غَيْرَكَ، قَالَ: قُلْ: آمَنْتُ بِاللَّهِ ثُمَّ اسْتَقِمْ.

رَوَاهُ مُسْلِمٌ.

21. ISTIQAMAH – GOING STRAIGHT

Abu 'Amr, and it is said Abu 'Amrah, Sufyan ibn 'Abdullah[i] ﷺ said, "I said, 'Messenger of Allah, say to me something on Islam about which I will not ask anyone other than you.' He said, 'Say, "I believe in Allah" then go straight.'" Muslim narrated it.

Commentary

His ﷺ saying, "Say, 'I believe in Allah' then go straight" [means]

---

[i] Abu 'Amr was called ath-Thaqafi because of his relationship to Thaqeef. He has also been called at-Ta'ifi because he is numbered among the people of at-Ta'if. 'Umar ﷺ appointed him to collect the *zakah* of at-Ta'if. He narrated five hadith.

as you have been commanded and forbidden. *Istiqamah*[i] (to go straight) is persevering in the path by doing what is obligatory and leaving what is forbidden. Allah says, *"Go straight as you have been commanded, and also those who turn*[ii] *with you* [to Allah].*"*[72] He said, *"The angels descend on those who say, 'Our Lord is Allah,' and then go straight"*[73] i.e. at death, giving them good news in His words, *"Do not fear and do not grieve, and rejoice in the Garden which you have been promised."*[74] In the commentary it is said that when they are given good news of the Garden they say, "And our children, what will they eat and what will their state be after us?" It will be said to them, *"We are your protectors in the life of the dunya*[iii] *and the akhirah,"*[75] i.e. "we (the angels) will look after their affairs after you, so let your eyes be at rest about that."

---

[i] *Istiqamah* derives from *qama* – 'he stood' and thus can possibly be understood as 'upstanding' or 'upright', but in the form *mustaqeem* is most often explained as that path 'which has no crookedness in it', i.e. 'straight'.

[ii] *Tawbah* – 'turning' has degrees the first of which is to turn from *kufr* and *shirk* to *iman*, the second of which is to turn from acts of disobedience to acts of obedience, and the highest of which is to turn from other than Allah to Allah alone.

[iii] *Dunya*, which is often translated as 'the world', is a feminine adjective meaning 'lower' or 'nearer', it qualifies the noun 'life' as in this *ayah*, 'the lower life' *al-hayat ad-dunya*, and is opposed to *akhirah* the 'later' [abode] *ad-dar al-akhirah*. It is often used as if it were a substantive.

الحديث الثاني والعشرون

عَنْ أَبِي عَبْدِ اللَّهِ جَابِرِ بْنِ عَبْدِ اللَّهِ الْأَنْصَارِيِّ رَضِيَ اللَّهُ عَنْهُمَا: أَنَّ رَجُلًا سَأَلَ رَسُولَ اللَّهِ ﷺ فَقَالَ: أَرَأَيْتَ إِذَا صَلَّيْتُ الْمَكْتُوبَاتِ، وَصُمْتُ رَمَضَانَ، وَأَحْلَلْتُ الْحَلَالَ، وَحَرَّمْتُ الْحَرَامَ، وَلَمْ أَزِدْ عَلَى ذَلِكَ شَيْئًا؛ أَأَدْخُلُ الْجَنَّةَ؟ قَالَ: نَعَمْ.

رَوَاهُ مُسْلِمٌ.

22. The Obligations

Abu 'Abdullah Jabir ibn 'Abdullah al-Ansari[i] ﷺ said, "A man asked the Messenger of Allah ﷺ saying, 'What do you think, if I pray the obligatory prayers, fast Ramadan,

---

[i] Jabir was one of the great companions, and his father 'Abdullah died as a *shaheed* at the battle of Uhud. The Prophet ﷺ said to Jabir, "My son, shall I not give you the good news that Allah, mighty is He and majestic, has brought your father to life and said, 'What do you wish?' He said, 'O my Lord, that you should return my spirit and send me back to the world so that I can be killed again.' He said, 'I have decreed that they (the dead) do not return to it (the world).'" His father died leaving a debt, so the Prophet ﷺ sought forgiveness of Allah on Jabir's ﷺ behalf twenty-seven times in one night for Him to discharge the debt of his father. Jabir died in Madinah in 73 AH when

and consider *halal* that which is *halal* and consider *haram* that which is *haram*, and I do not add anything to that, shall I enter the Garden?' He said, 'Yes.'" Muslim narrated it. The meaning of "I consider *haram* that which is *haram*" is "I avoid it", and the meaning of "I consider *halal* that which is *halal*" is "I do it believing that it is *halal*."

Commentary

His ﷺ saying, "What do you think?..." means "Tell me about...". His ﷺ saying, "...and I consider *halal* that which is *halal*" means "I believe that it is *halal* and of it I do that which is obligatory." "And I consider *haram* that which is *haram*" means "I believe that it is *haram* and I do not do it." His ﷺ saying, "Yes" means "You will enter the Garden."[i]

---

he was ninety-four years old. 1,540 hadith are narrated from him.

[i] If a Muslim man or woman fulfils their obligatory duties of praying the five prayers, paying the *zakah*, fasting Ramadan and performing the Hajj if they are able, then they are living a life of worship and service to Allah that no-one else in our age equals. As we have shown this requires of us to restore the pillar of *zakah* and the whole pattern of Islamic non-statist governance.

الحديث الثالث والعشرون

عَنْ أَبِي مَالِكٍ الْحَارِثِ بْنِ عَاصِمٍ الْأَشْعَرِيِّ ﷺ قَالَ: قَالَ رَسُولُ اللَّهِ ﷺ:

الطَّهُورُ شَطْرُ الْإِيمَانِ، وَالْحَمْدُ لِلَّهِ تَمْلَأُ الْمِيزَانَ، وَسُبْحَانَ اللَّهِ وَالْحَمْدُ لِلَّهِ تَمْلَآنِ - أَوْ: تَمْلَأُ - مَا بَيْنَ السَّمَاءِ وَالْأَرْضِ، وَالصَّلَاةُ نُورٌ، وَالصَّدَقَةُ بُرْهَانٌ، وَالصَّبْرُ ضِيَاءٌ، وَالْقُرْآنُ حُجَّةٌ لَكَ أَوْ عَلَيْكَ، كُلُّ النَّاسِ يَغْدُو، فَبَائِعٌ نَفْسَهُ فَمُعْتِقُهَا أَوْ مُوبِقُهَا.

رَوَاهُ مُسْلِمٌ.

23. PURITY IS HALF OF IMAN

Abu Malik al-Harith ibn 'Asim al-Ash'ari[i] ﷺ said, "The Messenger of Allah ﷺ said, 'Purity is half of iman; al-hamdulillah fills the scales; subhan'Allah wa'l-

---

[i] Al-Ash'ari denotes a relationship to a tribe in the Yemen who are known as al-Ash'ariyyun. Abu Malik later lived in Egypt, and he died in the plague during the *khilafah* of 'Umar ibn al-Khattab ﷺ in 18 AH.

hamdulillah both fill – or fills – whatever is between heaven and earth; prayer is light; *sadaqah*[i] is proof; patience is radiant light; and the Qur'an is an argument for or against you. Everybody goes out in the morning and sells his self, then he either frees it from slavery or destroys it." Muslim narrated it.

Commentary

In his ﷺ saying, "Purity is half of *iman*," purity is explained by al-Ghazali as purity of the heart from malice, envy, spite, and all other sicknesses of the heart. That is because perfect *iman* is only completed by that. Whoever has the two *shahadahs* has obtained half [of *iman*]. Whoever purifies his heart from the remaining sicknesses has perfected his *iman*. Whoever does not purify his heart then his *iman* is defective. One of them said, "Whoever purifies his heart, does *wudu'* and *ghusl* and prays, enters the prayer with both purifications together. Whoever enters the prayer with purity of the limbs particularly, has entered with one of the two purifications, and Allah glorious and exalted is He, only looks at purity of heart, because of his ﷺ saying, 'Truly Allah does not look at your bodies nor at your outward forms but He looks at your hearts.'"[76]

His ﷺ saying, "*Al-hamdulillah* fills the scales; *subhan'Allah wa'l-hamdulillah* both fill – or fills – whatever is between heaven and earth." This fills in the detail in another hadith, which is that Musa عليه السلام said to Allah, "My Lord, show me an action which will enter me into the Garden." He said, "Musa, say, 'There is no god but Allah', for if the seven heavens and seven earths were put in one pan of a scale and 'There is no god but Allah' in the other pan, 'There is no god but Allah' would be heavier." It is well known that the seven heavens and earths are the vastest things

---

[i] i.e. *zakah* and then optional acts of *sadaqah*.

between heaven and earth. Since *al-hamdulillah* fills the scale and more, *al-hamdulillah* must fill what is between heaven and earth, since the scale is vaster than that which is between heaven and earth and *al-hamdulillah* fills it. What is meant is that if it were a physical body it would fill it, or that the reward of *al-hamdulillah* would fill it.

His ﷺ saying, "Prayer is light" i.e. its reward is light. In another hadith there is, "And give good news of complete light on the Day of Rising to those who walk in darkness to the mosques."[i]

His ﷺ saying, "Sadaqah is proof" i.e. proof of the soundness of *iman* of one who gives it, and it is named *sadaqah* because it is a proof of the truthfulness (*sidq*) of his *iman*. That is because the hypocrite may pray but usually *sadaqah* is not easy for him.[ii]

His ﷺ saying, "Patience is radiant light" i.e. the beloved patience which is patience in obedience to Allah, and in the trials and abhorrent things of worldly life. Its meaning is that its (patience's) possessor will continue to be in the right [way].

The meaning of his ﷺ saying, "Everybody goes out in the morning and sells his self" is that every human strives for his self, and some of them sell it to Allah through obedience to Him and so free it from torment, and some of them sell it to shaytan and to whims by following the two of them "and so destroy it", i.e. make it perish. He ﷺ said, "Whoever says when he enters morning or evening: 'O Allah, I have entered upon the morning calling on You to witness and calling on the bearers of Your throne to witness, and Your angels and Your prophets and all of

---

[i] Abu Dawud and at-Tirmidhi transmitted it.

[ii] The historically important instance of this was the refusal of the Arabs to pay the *zakah* to the *Khalifah* Abu Bakr ﷺ. Even though they continued to affirm that they were Muslims and that they would perform the prayers, Abu Bakr ﷺ insisted on fighting them and that is the ruling up to this day, that war is waged on those who refuse to pay the *zakah*. See in hadith number 14 Imam an-Nawawi's commentary on the reasons for which a Muslim may be killed.

Your creation, that truly You, You are Allah, there is no god but You alone, no partner to You, and that Muhammad is Your slave and Your prophet', then Allah will free a quarter of him from the Fire, if he says it twice Allah will free a half of him from the Fire, if he says it three times Allah will free three quarters of him from the Fire, and if he says it four times Allah will free all of him from the Fire."

If it is said, "If the owner frees part of his slave the freeing passes to the rest of him, and Allah ﷻ has freed the first quarter but then it did not extend over him and similarly the rest", then the answer is that the extension is compulsory and compulsory things do not affect Allah ﷻ as opposed to others, and that which He does not will, does not happen in His judgement.

Allah ﷻ says, *"Allah has bought from the mu'minun their selves and their wealth..."*[i] One of the people of knowledge said, "No nobler sale than this has ever occurred. That is because the buyer is Allah and the sellers are the believers, the sale is their selves and the price is the Garden." In the *ayah* there is an indication that a seller is first of all compelled to surrender the goods before he receives the price, and that a buyer is not compelled first of all to surrender the price. That is because Allah ﷻ made *jihad* a duty on believers even to the extent that they are killed in the way of Allah and so He made it obligatory on them that they surrender the selves which have been sold, and [then] take the Garden.

If it is said, "How can the Master buy from His slaves their selves, and their selves are His property?" It is said, "He wrote them a contract for them to purchase their freedom and then He bought from them. Allah ﷻ made five prayers and fasting, etc.,

---

[i] Surat at-Tawbah: 111. *"Allah has bought from the mu'minun their selves and their wealth in return for the Garden. They fight in the Way of Allah and they kill and are killed. It is a promise binding on Him in the Torah, the Injil and the Qur'an and who is truer to his contract than Allah? Rejoice then in the bargain you have made. That is the great victory."*

obligatory on them, and when they do that they are free [and so then they can sell their selves for the Garden], and Allah ﷻ knows best."

الحديث الرابع والعشرون

عَنْ أَبِي ذَرٍّ الغِفَارِيِّ ﷺ عَنِ النَّبِيِّ ﷺ فِيمَا يَرْوِيهِ عَنْ رَبِّهِ تَبَارَكَ وَتَعَالَى، أَنَّهُ قَالَ:

يَا عِبَادِي إِنِّي حَرَّمْتُ الظُّلْمَ عَلَى نَفْسِي، وَجَعَلْتُهُ بَيْنَكُمْ مُحَرَّمًا، فَلَا تَظَالَمُوا. يَا عِبَادِي كُلُّكُمْ ضَالٌّ إِلَّا مَنْ هَدَيْتُهُ، فَاسْتَهْدُونِي أَهْدِكُمْ. يَا عِبَادِي كُلُّكُمْ جَائِعٌ إِلَّا مَنْ أَطْعَمْتُهُ، فَاسْتَطْعِمُونِي أُطْعِمْكُمْ. يَا عِبَادِي كُلُّكُمْ عَارٍ إِلَّا مَنْ كَسَوْتُهُ، فَاسْتَكْسُونِي أَكْسُكُمْ. يَا عِبَادِي إِنَّكُمْ تُخْطِئُونَ بِاللَّيْلِ وَالنَّهَارِ، وَأَنَا أَغْفِرُ الذُّنُوبَ جَمِيعًا؛ فَاسْتَغْفِرُونِي أَغْفِرْ لَكُمْ. يَا عِبَادِي إِنَّكُمْ لَنْ تَبْلُغُوا ضُرِّي فَتَضُرُّونِي، وَلَنْ تَبْلُغُوا نَفْعِي فَتَنْفَعُونِي. يَا عِبَادِي لَوْ أَنَّ أَوَّلَكُمْ وَآخِرَكُمْ

24. Injustice

وَإِنْسَكُمْ وَجِنَّكُمْ كَانُوا عَلَى أَتْقَى قَلْبِ رَجُلٍ وَاحِدٍ مِنْكُمْ مَا زَادَ ذَلِكَ فِي مُلْكِي شَيْئًا. يَا عِبَادِي لَوْ أَنَّ أَوَّلَكُمْ وَآخِرَكُمْ وَإِنْسَكُمْ وَجِنَّكُمْ كَانُوا عَلَى أَفْجَرِ قَلْبِ رَجُلٍ وَاحِدٍ مِنْكُمْ مَا نَقَصَ ذَلِكَ مِنْ مُلْكِي شَيْئًا. يَا عِبَادِي لَوْ أَنَّ أَوَّلَكُمْ وَآخِرَكُمْ وَإِنْسَكُمْ وَجِنَّكُمْ قَامُوا فِي صَعِيدٍ وَاحِدٍ فَسَأَلُونِي، فَأَعْطَيْتُ كُلَّ وَاحِدٍ مَسْأَلَتَهُ، مَا نَقَصَ ذَلِكَ مِمَّا عِنْدِي إِلَّا كَمَا يَنْقُصُ الْمِخْيَطُ إِذَا أُدْخِلَ الْبَحْرَ. يَا عِبَادِي إِنَّمَا هِيَ أَعْمَالُكُمْ أُحْصِيهَا لَكُمْ ثُمَّ أُوَفِّيكُمْ إِيَّاهَا، فَمَنْ وَجَدَ خَيْرًا فَلْيَحْمَدِ اللَّهَ، وَمَنْ وَجَدَ غَيْرَ ذَلِكَ فَلَا يَلُومَنَّ إِلَّا نَفْسَهُ.

رَوَاهُ مُسْلِمٌ.

24. Injustice

Abu Dharr al-Ghifari ﷺ narrated from the Prophet ﷺ in that which he narrated from his Lord, mighty is He and majestic, that He said, "My slaves, I have forbidden injustice to Myself and have forbidden it between you, so do not wrong each other. My slaves, all of you are astray except for whomever I guide, so seek guidance from Me, I will guide you. My slaves, all of you are hungry except for whomever I feed, so ask Me to feed you, I will feed you. My slaves, all of you are naked except for whomever I clothe, so seek clothing from Me, I will clothe you. My slaves, truly you miss the way by night and day and I forgive[i] wrong actions altogether, so ask for My forgiveness; I will forgive you. My slaves, you can not reach My harm so that you could harm Me, and you can never attain My benefit so that you could benefit Me. My slaves, even if the first and last of you, your human beings and your Jinn were according to the most God-fearing heart of any one man among you, that would not increase anything in My kingdom. My slaves, even if the first and last of you, your human beings and your Jinn were according to the most wicked heart of any one man among you, that would not decrease anything in My kingdom. My slaves, even if the first and last of you, your human beings and your Jinn were to stand on one flat piece of land and they were to ask Me and I gave each one of them what he asked for, that would not decrease what I have except as the needle does when it is entered into the sea. My slaves, they are only your actions which I enumerate for you, then later I will repay you for them. So whoever finds good then let

---

[i] *"Ghafara"* – literally "he covered" here translated as "He forgave" means that "He covered over [the wrong action for] the slave", so that he does not see it in his reckoning.

him praise Allah, and whoever finds other than that then let him not blame anyone but himself." Muslim narrated it.

Commentary

His saying, mighty is He and majestic, "Truly I have forbidden Myself injustice" i.e. "I am too far removed from it [as an impurity]", and injustice is inconceivable with respect to Allah ﷻ for injustice is going past the limit[i] and becoming occupied in the property of another[ii] which are both impossible with respect to Allah, exalted is He.

His ﷻ saying, "Do not wrong each other" i.e. none of you should do injustice to others.

In His ﷻ saying, "My slaves, you miss the way by night and day," *takhta'una* with a *fathah* (a) on the *ta* on the basis that it derives from *khati'a* "he did wrong or committed a mistake", which has a *fathah* on the *kha* and a *kasrah* on the *ta* and which in the imperfect tense is *yakhta'u*. It is permitted to have a *dammah* (u) on the *ta* [of *tukhti'una*] on the basis that it is from [the fourth form of the verb which is] *akhta'a* "he missed or failed to hit it (for example, the archer failed to hit the target)". [The word] *khata'a* "a wrong action, mistake or error" is used for [an act done] intentionally or through forgetfulness, and it is not sound to deny this linguistic understanding, and His words ﷻ refute it: *"Killing them is a terrible mistake (khata'an),"*[77] and it has also been recited as *khit'an*.

[About] His ﷻ saying, "My slaves, even if the first and last of you, your human beings and your Jinn..." traditional and

---

[i] Allah is exalted beyond limits.
[ii] Man owns nothing and is properly a *khalifah* who stands in on behalf of the King in His kingdom, his own life and body being gifts to him which he looks after as a steward on behalf of the King until the King requires them to be returned to Him. It is said that when Muslims are *khalifahs* in this sense, they will understand the reality of *khilafah* in the sense of governance.

intellectual proofs show that Allah is independent in His essence of everything, and that He ﷻ does not increase in abundance because of anything of His creations. Allah ﷻ has made clear that He has the kingdom of the heavens and earth and what is in between them, then He has made clear that He is in no need of that. Allah ﷻ says, *"He creates whatever He wills"*[78] and He is able to do away with this existence and to create other than it. Whoever is able to create every thing is in no need of any existent. Moreover, He glorious and exalted is He, made clear that He is in no need of a partner, so He ﷻ said, *"He has no partner in the Kingdom."*[79] Moreover, He ﷻ has made clear that He is independent and has no need of a helper or assistant, so He ﷻ says, *"Who needs no one to protect Him from abasement"*,[80] so the attribute of might is firmly established and endless for Him, and the attribute of abasement is prohibited for Him, exalted is He. Whoever is like that is in no need of the obedience of the obedient. Even if all people obeyed with the obedience of the most God-fearing man among them and hastened to obey His commands and prohibitions and did not oppose Him, He, glorious is He and exalted, would not boast of that abundance and that would not be an increase in His kingdom. Indeed their obedience is only attained by His grace and help, and their obedience is His blessing upon them. Even if all of them were to disobey Him with the disobedience of the most wicked of men, Iblis, and if they were to oppose His commands and prohibitions, that would not harm Him and it would not decrease anything of the perfection of His kingdom. For if He wished He would destroy them and create others. Glory be to the One who is not benefitted by obedience nor harmed by disobedience.

His ﷺ saying, "...and I were to give each one of them what he asked for, that would not decrease what I have, except as a needle does when it is entered into the sea" and it is well known that a needle does not visibly decrease the ocean at all, and that which is attached to a needle does not appear to have any visible trace, nor [any trace] in the scales.

His ﷺ saying, "Whoever finds good, then let him praise Allah" i.e. for his good grace in being guided to His obedience.

His ﷺ saying, "Whoever finds other than that, then let him blame no one but his self", since he gave it its desire and followed its whims.

الحديث الخامس والعشرون

عَنْ أَبِي ذَرٍّ ﷺ أَيْضًا:

أَنَّ نَاسًا مِنْ أَصْحَابِ رَسُولِ اللَّهِ ﷺ قَالُوا لِلنَّبِيِّ ﷺ يَا رَسُولَ اللَّهِ ذَهَبَ أَهْلُ الدُّثُورِ بِالْأُجُورِ؛ يُصَلُّونَ كَمَا نُصَلِّي، وَيَصُومُونَ كَمَا نَصُومُ، وَيَتَصَدَّقُونَ بِفُضُولِ أَمْوَالِهِمْ. قَالَ: أَوَلَيْسَ قَدْ جَعَلَ اللَّهُ لَكُمْ مَا تَصَّدَّقُونَ؟ إِنَّ بِكُلِّ تَسْبِيحَةٍ صَدَقَةً، وَكُلِّ تَكْبِيرَةٍ صَدَقَةً، وَكُلِّ تَحْمِيدَةٍ صَدَقَةً، وَكُلِّ تَهْلِيلَةٍ صَدَقَةً، وَأَمْرٌ بِمَعْرُوفٍ صَدَقَةٌ، وَنَهْيٌ عَنْ مُنْكَرٍ صَدَقَةٌ، وَفِي بُضْعِ أَحَدِكُمْ صَدَقَةٌ. قَالُوا يَا رَسُولَ اللَّهِ أَيَأْتِي أَحَدُنَا شَهْوَتَهُ وَيَكُونُ لَهُ فِيهَا أَجْرٌ؟ قَالَ: أَرَأَيْتُمْ لَوْ وَضَعَهَا فِي حَرَامٍ أَكَانَ عَلَيْهِ وِزْرٌ؟ فَكَذَلِكَ إِذَا وَضَعَهَا فِي الْحَلَالِ، كَانَ لَهُ أَجْرٌ.

رَوَاهُ مُسْلِمٌ.

25. THE WEALTHY AND THE POOR

Abu Dharr ❦ also narrated that, "Some people from the Companions of the Messenger of Allah said to the Prophet ❦, 'Messenger of Allah, the people of great wealth have gone off with the rewards. They pray as we pray, fast as we fast, and pay the *zakah*[i] with the excess of their properties.' He said, 'Has Allah not given you that with which you can give *sadaqah*? Truly, in every glorification there is *sadaqah*, in every magnification (*takbir*) there is *sadaqah*, every praise is *sadaqah*, in every "There is no god but Allah" there is *sadaqah*, in every command to the good there is *sadaqah*, in every forbidding of the wrong there is *sadaqah* and in every act of sexual intercourse by any of you there is *sadaqah*.' They said, 'Messenger of Allah, can one of us approach his appetite and have a reward for it?' He said, 'What do you think, if he had put it into something *haram* would there not have been a wrong [written] against him? Similarly if he puts it in the *halal* there is a reward for him.'" Muslim narrated it.

Commentary

His saying, "They said, 'Messenger of Allah, can one of us approach his appetite and have a reward for it?' He ❦ said, 'What do you think, if he had put it into something *haram* would there not have been a wrong [written] against him?'" Know that the appetite for sexual intercourse is one which the prophets and people of right action love, they say for those benefits of the

---

[i] *Yatasaddaqun*, from *sadaqa*: it is clear that the *sadaqah* referred to here refers firstly to the obligatory *zakah*, because the wealthy are enabled to pay *zakah* and more, and secondly to optional acts of generosity, since the poor have the option of extra voluntary acts, but do not attain the level of having to pay *zakah*, and Allah knows best.

deen and the world which are in it: lowering the eye, breaking the appetite so that one does not approach adultery, and gaining children by whom populating the world and the increase of the Ummah until the Day of Rising are made complete.[i] They say that involvement with all other appetites hardens the heart except for this one, for it softens the heart.

---

[i] Assumed in this understanding is that multiple-wife families are sunnah, but that it is permissible for a man to have one wife. This is the contrary of the modern misunderstanding that multiple-wife families are only acceptable in extraordinary situations of *jihad* and the like.

الحديث السادس والعشرون

عَنْ أَبِي هُرَيْرَةَ ﷺ قَالَ: قَالَ رَسُولُ اللَّهِ ﷺ:

كُلُّ سُلَامَى مِنَ النَّاسِ عَلَيْهِ صَدَقَةٌ، كُلَّ يَوْمٍ تَطْلُعُ فِيهِ الشَّمْسُ، تَعْدِلُ بَيْنَ اثْنَيْنِ صَدَقَةٌ، وَتُعِينُ الرَّجُلَ فِي دَابَّتِهِ فَتَحْمِلُهُ عَلَيْهَا أَوْ تَرْفَعُ لَهُ عَلَيْهَا مَتَاعَهُ صَدَقَةٌ، وَالْكَلِمَةُ الطَّيِّبَةُ صَدَقَةٌ، وَبِكُلِّ خُطْوَةٍ تَمْشِيهَا إِلَى الصَّلَاةِ صَدَقَةٌ، وَتُمِيطُ الْأَذَى عَنِ الطَّرِيقِ صَدَقَةٌ.

رَوَاهُ الْبُخَارِيُّ وَمُسْلِمٌ.

26. SADAQAH

Abu Hurairah ﷺ said, "The Messenger of Allah ﷺ said, 'Every member of every person owes *sadaqah* each day in which the sun rises. To exercise justice between two people is *sadaqah*, to help a man with his beast, to help him to mount it, or to lift his goods up to him when he is on it is *sadaqah*, a good word is *sadaqah*, every step with which you walk to prayer [in the mosque] is *sadaqah*, and to remove some harm from the road is *sadaqah*." Al-Bukhari and Muslim narrated it.

Commentary

His ﷺ saying, "Every member *(sulama)*[i] of every person owes *sadaqah* each day", and the *sulama* here are the members of the human body and it has been mentioned that there are three hundred and sixty members each of which owes a *sadaqah* every day. Every act of good, glorification, declaration of "There is no god but Allah", magnification, or every step which one takes to prayer is *sadaqah*. Whoever performs two *rak'ats* at the beginning of his day has paid the *zakah* on his body and so preserves the remainder of it. It has been narrated in the hadith literature that, "Two *rak'ats* of ad-Duha (the optional mid-morning prayer) stand in place of all of that."[81] In the hadith literature there is that "Allah ﷻ says, 'Son of Adam, pray four *rak'ats* at the beginning of the day and I will suffice you at the beginning of the day and I will suffice you at the end of it.'"[82]

---

[i] A word which encompasses organs, limbs and bones.

الحديث السابع والعشرون

عَنِ النَّوَّاسِ بْنِ سَمْعَانَ ﷺ عَنِ النَّبِيِّ ﷺ قَالَ: الْبِرُّ حُسْنُ الْخُلُقِ، وَالْإِثْمُ مَا حَاكَ فِي صَدْرِكَ، وَكَرِهْتَ أَنْ يَطَّلِعَ عَلَيْهِ النَّاسُ.

رواه مسلم.

وَعَنْ وَابِصَةَ بْنِ مَعْبَدٍ ﷺ قَالَ: أَتَيْتُ رَسُولَ اللهِ ﷺ فَقَالَ: جِئْتَ تَسْأَلُ عَنِ الْبِرِّ؟ قُلْتُ: نَعَمْ. فَقَالَ: اِسْتَفْتِ قَلْبَكَ، الْبِرُّ مَا اطْمَأَنَّتْ إِلَيْهِ النَّفْسُ، وَاطْمَأَنَّ إِلَيْهِ الْقَلْبُ، وَالْإِثْمُ مَا حَاكَ فِي النَّفْسِ وَتَرَدَّدَ فِي الصَّدْرِ، وَإِنْ أَفْتَاكَ النَّاسُ وَأَفْتَوْكَ.

حَدِيثٌ حَسَنٌ، رَوَيْنَاهُ فِي مُسْنَدَيِ الْإِمَامَيْنِ أَحْمَدَ بْنِ حَنْبَلٍ، وَالدَّارِمِيِّ بِإِسْنَادٍ حَسَنٍ.

27. Birr and Ithm

An-Nawwas ibn Sam'an narrated that the Prophet said, "*Birr*[i] is good nature, and *ithm*[ii] is that which becomes agitated[iii] in your self and which you would hate for people to discover." Muslim narrated it.

From Wabisah ibn Ma'bad that he said, "I came to the Messenger of Allah and he said, 'You have come to ask about *birr*?' I said, 'Yes!' He said, 'Ask your heart for a judgement. *Birr* is that towards which the self is tranquil and towards which the heart is tranquil. *Ithm* is that which becomes agitated in the self and it goes agitatedly to and fro in the breast even though people repeatedly give you a judgement [as to a matter's permissibility].'" A good hadith which we have narrated in the two *Musnads* of the Imams Ahmad ibn Hanbal and ad-Darimi with a good *isnad*.

Commentary

His saying, "*Birr* is good nature" and we have spoken before on good nature. Ibn 'Umar said, "*Birr* is a simple matter: a cheerful face and a soft tongue." Allah mentioned an *ayah* which gathered together all the types of *birr* when He says,

---

[i] The Arabic word is used here, because a point made clear by these two hadith is that *birr* and *ithm* were words which caused some difficulties even to Arabs, difficulties which they had to resolve by asking the Messenger of Allah to explain them. '*Birr*' derives from the word for 'land' as opposed to 'sea' and is said to contain the ideas of amplitude and extensiveness as well as good treatment and solicitous concern for others. It is held to be a quality which encompasses good behaviour towards Allah, parents and strangers.

[ii] *Ithm* could indeed be translated as 'guilt'.

[iii] *Haka*, the root of which is 'to become woven', the Imam later explains to mean 'to go agitatedly to and fro' perhaps like the weaver passing the weft back and forwards across the warp.

"*Rather, those with true devoutness [birr] are those who have iman in Allah and the Last Day...*"[83]

His ﷺ saying, "*Ithm is that which becomes agitated in your self*" i.e. it becomes agitated and it goes agitatedly to and fro, and the self is not at ease about doing it. In the hadith there is a proof that man must consult his heart when he wants to embark on an action, so then if the self is at ease with it he must do it, and if it is not at ease he must leave it alone. We have previously spoken about ambivalent doubt with respect to the hadith: "The *halal* is clear and the *haram* is clear."

It is narrated that Adam ﷺ gave his sons some parting advice, of which there is that he said, "If you want to do something, then if your hearts are agitated, do not do it, for when I drew near to eating from the tree my heart was agitated at eating." Of them there is also that he said, "If you want to do something then look at its consequences, for if I had looked at the consequences of eating, I would not have eaten from the tree." Of them there is that he said, "If you want to do something take the advice of experienced people, for if I had taken the advice of the angels, they would have advised me not to eat from the tree."

His ﷺ saying, "*...and which you would hate for people to discover*" is because people blame a man for eating that about which there is some doubt and for receiving that about which there is doubt and for marrying a woman about whom it has been said, "She was suckled along with him."[i] For this reason he ﷺ said, "How [can he do that]? when it is said..." Similarly with the *haram*, when a person receives it, he hates that people should discover him. Similar to the [situation with the] *haram* is consuming other people's property, for it is permitted [to him]

---

[i] Two children suckling from the same woman creates a sibling relationship between the two which prevents their marriage and either's marriage to any of the other's brothers, sisters, parents, sons, daughters, aunts and uncles, etc., as if they were genuinely brother and sister.

if he had ascertained that [the other] was contented with that, but if he has some doubt as to whether he is contented, then it is forbidden to consume it. Similarly, spending something entrusted to one without permission of its owner, because if people came to discover it they would reject that, and one hates that people should come to discover it because they would express their disapproval.

His ﷺ saying, "That which becomes agitated in the self ... even though people repeatedly give you a judgement", for example the gift which you receive from a person the majority of whose wealth is *haram*, and the self wavers agitatedly to and fro as to whether the gift is permissible, and a mufti gives you a judgement on the permissibility of consuming it, however the judgement does not remove ambivalent doubt. Similarly, when a woman informs a man that he was suckled along with so-and-so (the woman he intends to marry), then when the mufti gives judgement that it is permissible to marry her because of the lack of the proper number [of witnesses][i] the judgement will not remove doubt. Rather he must have caution even if people give him a judgement in his favour, and Allah knows best.

---

[i] A single witness is not enough, so while a single such witness would not be sufficient to prevent such a marriage it would raise a doubt.

الحديث الثامن والعشرون

عَنْ أَبِي نَجِيحٍ الْعِرْبَاضِ بْنِ سَارِيَةَ ﷺ قَالَ: وَعَظَنَا رَسُولُ اللهِ ﷺ مَوْعِظَةً وَجِلَتْ مِنْهَا الْقُلُوبُ، وَذَرَفَتْ مِنْهَا الْعُيُونُ، فَقُلْنَا يَا رَسُولَ اللهِ كَأَنَّهَا مَوْعِظَةُ مُوَدِّعٍ فَأَوْصِنَا، قَالَ أُوصِيكُمْ بِتَقْوَى اللهِ وَالسَّمْعِ وَالطَّاعَةِ وَإِنْ تَأَمَّرَ عَلَيْكُمْ عَبْدٌ، فَإِنَّهُ مَنْ يَعِشْ مِنْكُمْ فَسَيَرَى اخْتِلَافًا كَثِيرًا، فَعَلَيْكُمْ بِسُنَّتِي وَسُنَّةِ الْخُلَفَاءِ الرَّاشِدِينَ الْمَهْدِيِّينَ، عَضُّوا عَلَيْهَا بِالنَّوَاجِذِ، وَإِيَّاكُمْ وَمُحْدَثَاتِ الْأُمُورِ، فَإِنَّ كُلَّ بِدْعَةٍ ضَلَالَةٌ.

رَوَاهُ أَبُو دَاوُدَ، وَالتِّرْمِذِيُّ وَقَالَ: حَدِيثٌ حَسَنٌ صَحِيحٌ.

28. Taqwa of Allah, Hearing and Obedience

Abu Najih al-'Irbad ibn Sariyah[i] ﷺ said, "The Messenger of Allah ﷺ admonished us with an admonition by which the hearts became frightened and the eyes flowed with tears, so we said, 'Messenger of Allah, it is as if it were a farewell admonition, so advise us.' He said, 'I advise you to have *taqwa* of Allah, mighty is He and majestic, and to hear and obey even if a slave is given command over you. Whoever of you lives will see many disagreements, so you must take hold of my Sunnah and the Sunnah of rightly guided[ii] *khulafa'* who take the right way.[iii] Bite on it with the molar teeth. Beware of newly introduced matters, for every newly introduced matter is an innovation, and every innovation is a going astray.'"[iv] Abu

---

[i] He became a Muslim very early on. He was one of the people of the Suffah, the veranda of the mosque of the Prophet ﷺ and one of those who longed for the meeting with Allah. He died in Sham in 75 AH. He narrated thirty-one hadith.

[ii] *Mahdiyyeen* means 'rightly guided'.

[iii] *Rashidin* which I have translated as 'who took the right way' is often mistranslated as 'rightly guided' which has a passive sense, whereas it has an active meaning.

[iv] Ibn Taymiyyah said in his *Fatawa*: The Prophet ﷺ used to say, according to a *sahih* hadith, during the *khutbah* on the day of *Jumu'ah*: "The best speech is the speech of Allah, and the best guidance is the guidance of Muhammad ﷺ and the worse matters are those which are newly introduced and every innovation is an error," but he did not say: "And every error is in the Fire," for on the contrary, those who intend the truth may err from the truth although they have exerted themselves (in *ijtihad*) to find the right way in their quest but were incapable of it, and so will not be punished. They may do some of what they have been ordered to do and will thus have a reward for their exertion (*ijtihad*), whereas the mistake in which they erred from the reality of the matter is forgiven. Many of the people of *ijtihad* of the *salaf* and the later generations have said and done things that were innovation without knowing that they were innovations, either because of weak hadith which

Dawud and at-Tirmidhi narrated it and he [at-Tirmidhi] said, "A good *sahih* hadith."

Commentary

In his saying, "He admonished us", admonition is to cause fear.

In his saying, "…and from which the eyes flowed with tears" i.e. they wept and cried.

His ﷺ saying, "You must take hold of my Sunnah" i.e. "at the time of disagreements in affairs cling to my Sunnah."

"Bite on it with the molar teeth" which are the back teeth. It has been said, "The canine teeth."[i] When man bites with the molar teeth it is as if he gathers together [and bites with] all his teeth, so that it is a rhetorical device. A part of biting on the Sunnah is to take hold of it and not to follow the views of the people of caprice and innovations. *'addou* "bite!" is from *'adda* "he bit", *ya'addu* "he is biting/he bites", and it is with *fathah* (a) on the letter *'ayn*. Written with the *dammah* ('u' i.e. *'uddu*!) it is a mistake. For that reason you say, "Treat your mother with good nature (*barra*), Zayd!" which is from *barra* "he treated with good nature", *yabarru* "he treats with good nature" and you do not say *burra*! with a *dammah* (u) on the *ba*.

"And the Sunnah of rightly guided *khulafa'* who take the right way" meaning the four, who are: Abu Bakr, 'Umar, 'Uthman and 'Ali ﷺ.

---

they thought to be *sahih* or because of *ayats* from which they understood something that was not meant by them or because of a view they held on the matter whereas there were texts on the issue that had not reached them. When a man fears his Lord as much as he is able then he is comprised in His saying: "*Our Lord do not take us to task if we forget or make a mistake*" (Surat al-Baqarah: 285). And there is in the *Sahih* that Allah said: "I have done so."

[i] It has also been said that the wisdom teeth are meant.

الحديث التاسع والعشرون

عَنْ مُعَاذِ بْنِ جَبَلٍ ﷺ قَالَ:

قُلْتُ يَا رَسُولَ اللهِ أَخْبِرْنِي بِعَمَلٍ يُدْخِلُنِي الْجَنَّةَ وَيُبَاعِدُنِي مِنَ النَّارِ، قَالَ: لَقَدْ سَأَلْتَ عَنْ عَظِيمٍ، وَإِنَّهُ لَيَسِيرٌ عَلَى مَنْ يَسَّرَهُ اللهُ عَلَيْهِ: تَعْبُدُ اللهَ لَا تُشْرِكُ بِهِ شَيْئًا، وَتُقِيمُ الصَّلَاةَ، وَتُؤْتِي الزَّكَاةَ، وَتَصُومُ رَمَضَانَ، وَتَحُجُّ الْبَيْتَ، ثُمَّ قَالَ أَلَا أَدُلُّكَ عَلَى أَبْوَابِ الْخَيْرِ؟ الصَّوْمُ جُنَّةٌ، وَالصَّدَقَةُ تُطْفِئُ الْخَطِيئَةَ كَمَا يُطْفِئُ الْمَاءُ النَّارَ، وَصَلَاةُ الرَّجُلِ فِي جَوْفِ اللَّيْلِ، ثُمَّ تَلَا: تَتَجَافَى جُنُوبُهُمْ عَنِ الْمَضَاجِعِ ... حَتَّى بَلَغَ ... يَعْمَلُونَ، ثُمَّ قَالَ أَلَا أُخْبِرُكَ بِرَأْسِ الْأَمْرِ وَعَمُودِهِ وَذِرْوَةِ سَنَامِهِ؟ قُلْتُ بَلَى يَا رَسُولَ اللهِ. قَالَ رَأْسُ الْأَمْرِ الْإِسْلَامُ،

وَعَمُودُهُ الصَّلَاةُ، وَذِرْوَةُ سَنَامِهِ الْجِهَادُ، ثُمَّ قَالَ: أَلَا أُخْبِرُكَ بِمَلَاكِ ذَلِكَ كُلِّهِ؟ فَقُلْتُ: بَلَى يَا رَسُولَ اللَّهِ فَأَخَذَ بِلِسَانِهِ وَقَالَ: كُفَّ عَلَيْكَ هَذَا. قُلْتُ: يَا نَبِيَّ اللَّهِ وَإِنَّا لَمُؤَاخَذُونَ بِمَا تَتَكَلَّمُ بِهِ؟ فَقَالَ: ثَكِلَتْكَ أُمُّكَ وَهَلْ يَكُبُّ النَّاسَ عَلَى وُجُوهِهِمْ - أَوْ قَالَ عَلَى مَنَاخِرِهِمْ - إِلَّا حَصَائِدُ أَلْسِنَتِهِمْ؟

رَوَاهُ التِّرْمِذِيُّ وَقَالَ: حَدِيثٌ حَسَنٌ صَحِيحٌ.

29. A Comprehensive Hadith on Action

Mu'adh ibn Jabal said, "I said, 'Messenger of Allah tell me about an action which will enter me into the Garden and remove me far from the Fire.' He said, 'You have asked about a tremendous thing, and it is easy for one for whom Allah makes it easy: [it is] that you worship Allah without associating anything with Him, establish prayer, produce *zakah*, fast Ramadan, and perform Hajj of the House.' Then he said, 'Shall I not show you the doors of good? Fasting is a shield, and *sadaqah* extinguishes error as water extinguishes fire, and the prayer of a man in the middle of the night,' and then he recited, *'Their sides eschew their beds'* until he reached *'... what it used to do.*'ⁱ Then he said, 'Shall I not tell you about the head of the matter, its central pillar and the uppermost part of its hump?' I said, 'Yes, Messenger of Allah.' He ﷺ said, 'The head of the matter is Islam, and its central pillar is prayer, and the summit of its hump is *jihad*.' Then he said, 'Shall I not tell you of the foundation (*milak*) of all of that?' I said, 'Yes, Messenger of Allah.' He took hold of his tongue and said, 'Restrain this.' I said, 'Prophet of Allah, are we taken to task for what we talk about?' And he said, 'May your mother be bereft of you, Mu'adh! Does anything throw people into the Fire on their faces' – or he said, 'on their nostrils' – 'except the harvest of their tongues?'" At-Tirmidhi related it and said, "A good *sahih* hadith."

Commentary

His ﷺ saying, "…and the uppermost part of its hump" i.e. the highest part of it. The *milak* (foundation) of a thing, with *kasrah* (i) on the letter *mim*, i.e. its purpose. His ﷺ saying, "May your mother be bereft of you" i.e. "may she lose you", and the Messenger of Allah ﷺ did not intend the supplication literally, rather that it is a custom of the Arabs in conversation. The "harvest of their tongues" is their crimes against people by their attacking their honour and walking about with tales, etc. The crimes of the tongue are: backbiting, telling stories, lying, slander, the word of disbelief, mockery and breaking promises. Allah ﷻ says, "*It is deeply abhorrent to Allah that you should say what you do not do.*"[84]

ⁱ Surat as-Sajdah: 16-17. "*Their sides eschew their beds as they call on their Lord in fear and ardent hope. And they give of what We have provided for them. No self knows the delight that is hidden away for it in recompense for what it used to do.*"

الحديث الثلاثون

عَنْ أَبِي ثَعْلَبَةَ الْخُشَنِيِّ جُرْثُومِ بْنِ نَاشِبٍ ﷺ عَنْ رَسُولِ اللَّهِ ﷺ قَالَ:

إِنَّ اللَّهَ تَعَالَى فَرَضَ فَرَائِضَ فَلَا تُضَيِّعُوهَا، وَحَدَّ حُدُودًا فَلَا تَعْتَدُوهَا، وَحَرَّمَ أَشْيَاءَ فَلَا تَنْتَهِكُوهَا، وَسَكَتَ عَنْ أَشْيَاءَ رَحْمَةً لَكُمْ غَيْرَ نِسْيَانٍ فَلَا تَبْحَثُوا عَنْهَا.

حَدِيثٌ حَسَنٌ، رَوَاهُ الدَّارَقُطْنِيُّ، وَغَيْرُهُ.

30. Obligations and Limits

Abu Tha'labah al-Khushni Jurthum ibn Nashir[i] ﷺ narrated that the Messenger of Allah ﷺ said, "Truly Allah has made obligations obligatory so do not waste them, and He has defined limits so do not transgress them,

---

[i] He was one of the famous Companions and one of those who were present at the Pledge of Allegiance of ar-Ridwan underneath the tree in the sixth year of the *Hijrah*. He died in Sham in 95 AH. He narrated forty hadith.

and He has forbidden some things so do not violate them, and He was silent about some things as a mercy to you, not out of forgetfulness, so do not investigate them." A good hadith which ad-Daraqutni and others narrated.

Commentary

His ﷺ saying, "...and He has forbidden some things so do not violate them" i.e. do not enter into them.

The meaning of his ﷺ saying, "...and He was silent about some things as a mercy to you" has already been spoken about.

الحديث الحادي والثلاثون

عَنْ أَبِي الْعَبَّاسِ سَهْلِ بْنِ سَعْدٍ السَّاعِدِيِّ ﷺ قَالَ: جَاءَ رَجُلٌ إِلَى النَّبِيِّ ﷺ فَقَالَ:

يَا رَسُولَ اللَّهِ دُلَّنِي عَلَى عَمَلٍ إِذَا عَمِلْتُهُ أَحَبَّنِي اللَّهُ وَأَحَبَّنِي النَّاسُ، فَقَالَ: ازْهَدْ فِي الدُّنْيَا يُحِبَّكَ اللَّهُ، وَازْهَدْ فِيمَا عِنْدَ النَّاسِ يُحِبَّكَ النَّاسُ.

حديث حسن، رَوَاهُ ابْنُ مَاجَهْ، وغيرهُ بِأَسَانِيدَ حَسَنَةٍ.

31. ZUHD – DOING-WITHOUT

Abu'l-'Abbas Sahl ibn Sa'd as-Sa'idi[i] 🙵 said, "A man came to the Prophet 🙵 and said, 'Messenger of Allah, show me an action which if I do it, Allah will love me and people will love me.' He said, 'Do without the world and Allah will love you, and do without that which people have and people will love you.'" A good hadith which Ibn Majah and others narrated with good *isnads*.

---

[i] His name used to be Hazn (Rugged or Rough) and so the Prophet 🙵 named him Sahl (Smooth). The Prophet 🙵 died when Sahl was fifteen years old. He was the last of the Companions to die in Madinah, dying in 91 AH. He narrated 188 hadith.

Commentary

In his ﷺ saying, "Do without the world and Allah will love you", doing-without (*zuhd*) means leaving that of the world for which one has no need, even if it is *halal* and to confine oneself to sufficiency.[i] Scrupulousness (*wara'*) means to leave ambivalent things.

They say that the most intelligent of people are the people of doing-without, because they love what Allah loves and dislike amassing the world which Allah dislikes, and they employ rest for themselves. Ash-Shafi'i said, may Allah ﷻ show him mercy, "If a bequest had been made for the most intelligent of people, then it would have been turned to the people of doing-without."

One of them said:

> "Be one who does without that which men's hands possess
> you will become beloved to all of mankind.
> Do you not see the hunting bird is forbidden their provision
> so it becomes a leader, in the laps, [as if] a close relative?"[ii]

---

[i] Sufficiency must be understood in the context of the obligation of every Muslim man and woman to pay the *zakah*, which presupposes that, if possible, one will have untouched, for a year, the *nisab* upon which *zakah* becomes obligatory, i.e. twenty gold dinars, two hundred silver dirhams, and/or the requisite number of cattle, and/or the quantities of grain and dates, etc.

We live in an age of spectacular greed in which enormously voracious individuals devour the earth. At the other end of the scale a characteristic disease of the age is anorexia, the constant denial to oneself of much-needed nourishment and the perpetual attempt to reduce one's needs. All the statements on doing-without need to be understood somewhere well within these two extreme positions. The thought that it is possible to quietly live on a little *halal* income is becoming increasingly unlikely for the huge majority of the earth's population. Indeed a major struggle is needed to bring about any sort of *halal* economy within which anyone could have the luxury of living with the traditional virtues of *zuhd* (doing-without). For that there is needed an Islamic people, great numbers of whom each possess the *nisab* and pay the *zakah* on it, as opposed to the capitalist model of a few extraordinarily wealthy-through-enormous-debt individuals and families, and a great many indebted wage and salary earners.

[ii] The trained hunting bird is prevented from eating its prey, but it is honoured and has a place in the family.

31. Zuhd – Doing-Without

Ash-Shafi'i ﷺ said in blame of the world:
"Whoever tastes the world, then I have tasted it,
   its sweetness ('adhb) and its torment ('adhab) were driven to us,
but I only see it as a deception and falsehood,
   just as the mirage that appears in the middle of the waterless desert.
It is nothing but an absurd corpse,
   on which there are dogs who desire its enticements.
If you avoid it you will be peace to its people,
   but if you are enticed by it, its dogs will struggle with you.
Repulse the surpluses of affairs, for they are
   forbidden to embark on for the person of *taqwa*."

His saying, "Forbidden to embark on for the person of *taqwa*" shows that rejoicing in the world is forbidden, which al-Baghawi announced clearly in his commentary on His ﷺ words, "*They rejoice in the life of the dunya.*"[85] Moreover, what is meant by that which is blameworthy of the world is seeking more than sufficiency. As for seeking sufficiency that is obligatory. One of them said, "That is not worldly; the world is what is in excess over sufficiency" and he sought to prove it by His ﷺ saying, "*To mankind the love of worldly appetites is painted in glowing colours: women and children...*"[86] so that then His ﷺ saying indicates what was mentioned previously of seeking expansion [of the world rather than seeking what one needed of it]. Ash-Shafi'i said, may Allah ﷺ show him mercy, "Seeking increase in the *halal* is a punishment by which Allah tries the people of *tawhid*." One of them said:

"There is no house for the man after death in which he will live,
   Except for the one which before death he was building.
If he builds it well his dwelling will be pleasant,
   but if he builds it badly, its builder has failed.
The self desires the world and already knows,
   that doing-without in it is abandoning that which is in it.
Plant the roots of *taqwa* as long as you continue to exert yourself,
   and know that after death you will meet them."

Moreover, after that, if one rejoices in it because of boasting, competing and becoming insolent to people then that is blameworthy, but whoever rejoices in it because it is a part of the bounty of Allah upon him then that is praiseworthy. 'Umar ؓ said, "O Allah, we do not rejoice except in that which You provide us."

Allah ﷻ has praised those who are moderate[i] in their living and He ﷻ said, *"Those who, when they spend, are neither extravagant nor mean,"*[87] and he ﷺ said, "Whoever asks Allah to choose for him [with the *du'a* of *istikharah*] will not fail, whoever seeks advice will never regret, and whoever is moderate will never be in need."[88] It used to be said, "Moderation in the way of living suffices you for a half of provision." *Iqtisad* (moderation) is contentment with sufficiency. One of the people of right action said, "Whoever earns wholesomely [in a *halal* fashion] and spends with intention (or moderately), advances [for himself] a bounty."

---

[i] *Muqtasidin* and *iqtisad* are from the root *qasada* "he intended or purposed". The essential thought in *iqtisad* is to spend with intention and purpose, and thus 'moderately' and, as the *ayah* in Surat al-Furqan makes clear, in between the two extremes of extravagance and meanness. It is this significant word which has been twisted by being translated as 'economics' (a study which was regarded as a pseudo-science when introduced into Oxford University) and thus to the even more abhorrent 'Islamic Economics', an umbrella term for the innovation of Islamic Banking in order to introduce usury into the heart of the *shari'ah*.

الحديث الثاني والثلاثون

عَنْ أَبِي سَعِيدٍ سَعْدِ بْنِ مَالِكِ بْنِ سِنَانٍ الْخُدْرِيِّ ﷺ أَنَّ رَسُولَ اللَّهِ ﷺ قَالَ:

لَا ضَرَرَ وَلَا ضِرَارَ.

حَدِيثٌ حَسَنٌ، رَوَاهُ ابْنُ مَاجَهْ، وَالدَّارَقُطْنِيّ، وَغَيْرُهُمَا مُسْنَدًا. وَرَوَاهُ مَالِكٌ فِي "الْمُوَطَّإِ" عَنْ عَمْرِو بْنِ يَحْيَى عَنْ أَبِيهِ عَنِ النَّبِيِّ ﷺ مُرْسَلًا، فَأَسْقَطَ أَبَا سَعِيدٍ، وَلَهُ طُرُقٌ يُقَوِّي بَعْضُهَا بَعْضًا.

32. Causing Harm and Returning Harm

Abu Sa'id Sa'd ibn Malik ibn Sinan al-Khudri[i] ﷺ narrated that the Messenger of Allah ﷺ said, "There is [to be] no causing harm nor returning harm." It is a good hadith which Ibn Majah, ad-Daraqutni and others narrated with *isnads*.

---

[i] He went to battle along with the Messenger of Allah ﷺ twelve times. He was one of the great Companions and one of their men of knowledge. He was charged by Sayyiduna Abu Bakr ﷺ with the task of compiling the first copy of the Qur'an, and subsequently by Sayyiduna 'Uthman ﷺ with the job of preparing the edition upon which all other copies are now based. He died in Madinah in 74 AH when he was ninety-four years old, and is buried in al-Baqi'. He narrated 1,170 hadith.

Malik narrated it in the *Muwatta* in a *mursal*[i] form from 'Amr ibn Yahya from his father from the Prophet ﷺ and he omitted Abu Sa'id. It has different paths [of transmission] some of which reinforce others.

Commentary

His ﷺ saying, "There is [to be] no causing harm" i.e. let none of you cause harm to another without right nor [without it being in retaliation for] any previous injury [from the other party].

His ﷺ saying, "Nor returning harm" i.e. do not harm whoever harms you, and if someone abuses you do not abuse him, rather seek your rights from a judge without [returning the] abuse. If two men abuse each other or slander each other, let mutual retaliation not take place, but rather let each one take his due by means of a judge. In the hadith literature there is narrated from him ﷺ that he said, "Each of the two who abuse each other has what he said, and the one who began is in the wrong as long as the wronged one does not transgress with extra abuse."

---

[i] *Mursal* means narration of the hadith without mentioning the name of the Companion who is the ultimate source of transmission from the Prophet ﷺ. It is wrongly thought by modern Muslims that the *mursal* is intrinsically weak, but in the old practice hadith were sometimes transmitted as *mursal* because the narrator had them from more than one Companion, and to ascribe it to one Companion would have weakened his narration.

"Al-A'mash said, 'I said to Ibrahim [an-Nakha'i], 'Give me something from Ibn Mas'ud with a chain of transmission.' He said, 'If I narrate you something from a man from 'Abdullah that is what I heard. If I say, "Abdullah said..." then it is from more than one person.'" 'Abd al-Hayy al-Laknawi, *At-Ta'liq al-Mumajjad*.

الحديث الثالث والثلاثون

عَنْ ابْنِ عَبَّاسٍ رَضِيَ اللَّهُ عَنْهُمَا أَنَّ رَسُولَ اللَّهِ ﷺ قَالَ: لَوْ يُعْطَى النَّاسُ بِدَعْوَاهُمْ لَادَّعَى رِجَالٌ أَمْوَالَ قَوْمٍ وَدِمَاءَهُمْ، لَكِنَّ الْبَيِّنَةَ عَلَى الْمُدَّعِي، وَالْيَمِينَ عَلَى مَنْ أَنْكَرَ.

حَدِيثٌ حَسَنٌ، رَوَاهُ الْبَيْهَقِيُّ، وَغَيْرُهُ هَكَذَا، وَبَعْضُهُ فِي الصَّحِيحَيْنِ.

33. Claimants and Counter-Claimants

Ibn 'Abbas ؓ narrated that the Messenger of Allah ﷺ said, "If people were to be given according to what they claim, men would claim people's property and blood, but clear evidence is required of a claimant and an oath is required of someone who denies [the claim]." A good hadith which al-Bayhaqi and others related as above, and a part of it is in the two *Sahih* books.

Commentary

In his ﷺ saying, "Clear evidence is required of a claimant and an oath is required of someone who denies [the claim]," clear evidence is required of a claimant only because he claims something which contradicts the actual state of affairs, and one assumes innocence [on the part of a defendant] until guilt is proven.[i] Only an oath is required of one against whom a claim is made,[ii] because his claim accords with the actual state of affairs and he is considered innocent until proven guilty.

Some matters are excluded. A claimant without evidence is accepted with respect to that which can only be known by means of him:

i. Such as a father's claim that he needs to keep [his daughter] chaste [by insisting that she marry];

ii. The claim, supported by circumstantial evidence, of an impetuous and legally incompetent person [literally 'an idiot'] to [having contracted] a marriage [because such a person needs the consent of his guardian to contract a marriage];

iii. The claim of a hermaphrodite of [having either] feminine or masculine gender;

iv. A child's claim of having attained puberty through having had a wet dream;

v. A near relative's claim of his lack of property in order that he can take some maintenance;

vi. The claim of an indebted person of difficulty in [repaying] a debt which is binding on him and for which there is no direct (monetary) recompense, such as a dowry of a wife, warranty [i.e. for work done], and the [liability incurred for the] value of something destroyed;

---

[i] A translation of what is an almost telegraphic Arabic phrase which holds some of the meaning of English phrases such as "possession is nine-tenths of the law" etc.

[ii] He does not have to have evidence or proof.

33. Claimants and Counter-Claimants

vii. A woman's claim that her *'iddah* has come to an end, with her avowal [of the end of the periods of purity] or by her giving birth;

viii. Her claim that she has become eligible [for remarriage after the triple divorce from her first husband, because of her second husband having consummated the marriage] and that she has then been divorced [thus allowing her to remarry her first husband];

ix. The claim of one entrusted [with some goods] that the entrusted [goods] were destroyed, lost or stolen, etc.;

x. Similarly, the oath called *qasamah* [which is sworn fifty times by the relatives of a murdered man when there is not evidence of two witnesses to the murder][i] is excluded [from the need for clear evidence], because oaths are required of a claimant when there is suspicion;

xi. The divorce called *li'an*[ii] [is excluded too] for [in it] a husband slanders [his wife by accusing her of adultery without witnesses] and lays a curse on himself [if he is lying] and thus the *hadd* punishment [for slander] is dropped [from the husband];[iii]

xii. A [husband's] claim of sexual intercourse during a period of impotence, for if the woman denies him, the husband is believed in his claim unless the wife is a virgin;

xiii. Similarly if he claimed that he had intercourse with her in the period of sworn abstinence from intercourse;[iv]

---

[i] The accused may avert retaliation by fifty oaths of his innocence. See the *Muwatta* of Imam Malik, Book 44, the *Oath of Qasamah*.

[ii] In which a husband swears four oaths that his wife committed adultery and a fifth oath that the curse of Allah be upon him if he has lied, and she averts punishment from herself if she swears four oaths that she did not commit adultery and a fifth oath that the curse of Allah is upon her if she has lied. They are divorced and can never remarry in any circumstances.

[iii] Clear evidence in any accusation of adultery is a confession repeated four times, or the testimony of four trusted Muslim witnesses to the act of intercourse. Even if three such witnesses were to testify they would be flogged for slander.

[iv] If a man swears not to have intercourse with his wife and abstains for four

xiv. Similarly, one who abandons prayer, if he says that he prayed in the house, [he is not required to show clear evidence],

xv. Someone who refuses to pay *zakah* [to *zakah* collectors] if he says, "I paid it myself" except when the poor [who should have received his *zakah*] deny it and they are a limited number, then he must produce clear evidence;[i]

xvi. Similarly, someone who claims poverty and asks for *zakah* is given it and not made to swear an oath, as opposed to when he claims to have dependents, for that requires clear evidence;

xvii. If someone eats on the thirtieth day of Ramadan and claims that he saw the moon[ii] then that is not accepted from him if he claims it after eating, because he may only be trying to avert punishment from himself. If he claims that before eating, then it is accepted from him and he is not to be

---

months, he must then declare his intent or divorce her.

[i] Muslims are required to pay their *zakah* to the collectors appointed by the Amir. Ibn Juzayy says in the sub-heading of the chapter on *zakah* from *al-Qawanin al-Fiqhiyyah*, "It is an obligation and one of the pillars of Islam, and whoever denies that it is an obligation is a disbeliever, and whoever refuses it then it is taken from him by force, and if he resists it then he is to be fought until he pays it." Furthermore, he says, "If the Imam [the *Khalifah*] is just [i.e. he can be trusted to pay it to the categories permitted to receive it] it is obligatory to pay the *zakah* to him, and if he is not just but it is not possible to divert the payment of the *zakah* from him then it must be paid to him and that discharges the obligation. If it is possible to divert the payment of the *zakah* from him then the owner of it pays it to those who are worthy. It is then recommended that he not undertake the payment of it himself for fear of being praised for it."

[ii] The Muslim leader is the one to declare the beginning and the end of Ramadan. He does that on the advice of a *qadi* to whom Muslim witnesses have testified that they have seen the moon and the *qadi* is satisfied on examination that the witnesses are acceptable and the sighting is genuine. In the case of clear cloudless conditions, then the sighting must be a mass sighting by significant numbers of the population. If it is cloudy, then there arises the case of two just Muslim witnesses and their interrogation by the *qadi* to verify the authenticity of their evidence.

punished, but he ought to eat secretly, since his witnessing alone is not acceptable.[i]

In his ﷺ saying, "...and an oath is required of one who denies [a claim]", this oath is called "an oath of restraint (patience)" and "[an oath] which plunges [one who swears it falsely into serious wrong action and thus into the Fire]." It is called an oath of restraint (*sabr*) because it holds a possessor of a right back from his right, and holding back is a form of restraint. In that sense it is said of a person who has been killed and who is held back from burial that he is restrained.[ii] He ﷺ said, "Whoever swears a restraining oath, by which he cuts off the property of a Muslim man, and in which he has deviated from the truth, will meet Allah and He will be angry with him."[89]

This oath is only with respect to things past, and it occurs in many places in the Tremendous Qur'an, for example His ﷺ saying, *"They swear by Allah that they said nothing,"*[90] and of it there is His saying informing about the disbelievers, *"Then they will have no recourse except to say, 'By Allah, our Lord, We were not mushrikun.'"*[91] Another example of it is His ﷺ saying, *"Those who sell Allah's contract and their own oaths for a paltry price..."*[92] It is recommended that the judge should recite this *ayah* at the time of taking an oath from a disputant in order that he should abstain [from a false oath or one in which he has doubt].

---

[i] This is the position of ash-Shafi'i, but Malik and Ahmad ibn Hanbal say that the solitary person who sees the moon of Shawwal "does not break his fast, for fear of suspicion falling on him." From *al-Qawanin al-Fiqhiyyah* of Ibn Juzayy al-Kalbi.

According to the school of Malik, Ibn Juzayy said, "If he does break the fast there is nothing against him in that which is between him and Allah, however if he is discovered he is punished if he is suspected [of just trying to break the fast]." From *al-Qawanin al-Fiqhiyyah*.

[ii] i.e. *musabbar* from *sabr* 'patience'.

الحديث الرابع والثلاثون

عَنْ أَبِي سَعِيدٍ الْخُدْرِيِّ ﷺ قَالَ سَمِعْتُ رَسُولَ اللَّهِ ﷺ يَقُولُ: مَنْ رَأَى مِنْكُمْ مُنْكَرًا فَلْيُغَيِّرْهُ بِيَدِهِ، فَإِنْ لَمْ يَسْتَطِعْ فَبِلِسَانِهِ، فَإِنْ لَمْ يَسْتَطِعْ فَبِقَلْبِهِ، وَذَلِكَ أَضْعَفُ الْإِيمَانِ.

رَوَاهُ مُسْلِمٌ.

34. Seeing Something Objectionable

Abu Sa'id al-Khudri ﷺ said, "I heard the Messenger of Allah ﷺ saying, 'Whoever of you sees something objectionable then let him change it with his hand, and if he is not able then with his tongue, and if he is not able then with his heart, and that is the weakest *iman*.'" Muslim narrated it.

Commentary

It is not meant by his ﷺ saying, "...that is the weakest *iman*" that the one who is incapable [of strong action or words] has weaker *iman* than someone else. What is meant is only that that is the lowest of *iman*. That is because action is the fruit of *iman*,

34. Seeing Something Objectionable

and that the highest fruit of *iman*, in the realm of forbidding that which is objectionable, is to prevent it by hand, and then if he is killed he is a *shaheed*.[i] Allah ﷻ says, recounting the words of Luqman, *"My son, establish salat and command what is right and forbid what is wrong and be steadfast in the face of all that happens to you."*[93]

For one who is able, it is obligatory to forbid with the tongue even if he will not be listened to, just as when he knows that if he greets someone they will not return the greeting yet he must still greet [them].

If it is said that his ﷺ saying, "...and if he is not able then with his tongue, and if he is not able then with his heart" requires that one who is not able is not permitted to try and change [the wrong] with anything other than the heart, and that the command [here] signifies the obligation [to change it with the heart, rather than signifying recommendation], then the answer has two aspects:

First is that what is understood is further qualified by His ﷺ saying, "...*and be steadfast in the face of all that happens to you,*" (i.e. that he ought to act or speak out and then be patient with what happens to him as a result).

Second, is that the command [to change the wrong with the heart] removes the [guilt of] wrongdoing [from someone who did not actively change the wrong or speak against it] but it does not remove the recommendation [that it should be done with hand or tongue].

If it is said that denying it with the heart does not change the

---

[i] A *shaheed* is a witness, i.e. in the sense that he witnesses the truth and bears witness to it. The *shaheed* enters the Garden immediately on his death without resurrection and without awaiting the Reckoning. In fact, its meaning is identical, etymologically speaking, to the meaning of 'martyr', but regrettably the latter has come to mean someone who endures terrible pain passively and therefore is an unsuitable translation.

objectionable, so what is the meaning of his ﷺ saying, "...then [he must change it] by his heart"? (i.e. how can he 'change' it?), the answer to that is that he should reject it and not be contented with it, and he should occupy himself with remembrance of Allah. Allah ﷻ praises those who do that when He says, *"And who, when they pass by worthless talk, pass by with dignity."*[94]

الحديث الخامس والثلاثون

عَنْ أَبِي هُرَيْرَةَ ﷺ قَالَ: قَالَ رَسُولُ اللَّهِ ﷺ:

لَا تَحَاسَدُوا، وَلَا تَنَاجَشُوا، وَلَا تَبَاغَضُوا، وَلَا تَدَابَرُوا، وَلَا يَبِعْ بَعْضُكُمْ عَلَى بَيْعِ بَعْضٍ، وَكُونُوا عِبَادَ اللَّهِ إِخْوَانًا، الْمُسْلِمُ أَخُو الْمُسْلِمِ، لَا يَظْلِمُهُ، وَلَا يَخْذُلُهُ، وَلَا يَكْذِبُهُ، وَلَا يَحْقِرُهُ، التَّقْوَى هَاهُنَا، وَيُشِيرُ إِلَى صَدْرِهِ ثَلَاثَ مَرَّاتٍ، بِحَسْبِ امْرِئٍ مِنَ الشَّرِّ أَنْ يَحْقِرَ أَخَاهُ الْمُسْلِمَ، كُلُّ الْمُسْلِمِ عَلَى الْمُسْلِمِ حَرَامٌ: دَمُهُ وَمَالُهُ وَعِرْضُهُ.

رَوَاهُ مُسْلِمٌ.

35. Brotherhood

Abu Hurairah ﷺ said, "The Messenger of Allah ﷺ said, 'Do not envy each other, do not bid against each other, do not hate each other, do not turn your backs on each other, and let none of you sell upon the sale of another. Be slaves of Allah, brothers. A Muslim is the brother of a Muslim, he does not wrong him, fail to assist him, lie to him nor despise him. *Taqwa* is here" and he pointed to his breast with his hand three times. "It is sufficient evil for a man that he should despise his brother Muslim. All of a Muslim is sacred for a Muslim, his blood, his property and his honour." Muslim narrated it.

Commentary

About his ﷺ saying, "Do not envy each other", it has previously been mentioned that there are three types of envy.

Najash [from which derives "do not bid against each other"] means originally to raise and increase, and it is that someone increases the price of an article [by entering the bidding] because of jealousy of another, and it is forbidden because it is dishonest and deceitful.

His ﷺ saying, "Do not turn your backs on each other" [means] let none of you give up on his brother even if he sees him turning his back on him. He ﷺ said, "It is not permitted for a Muslim to forsake his brother for more than three nights, so that they meet and this one turns away and this one turns away. The best of the two of them is the first to greet."[95]

The form of the 'sale upon the sale of his brother' is that his brother should sell something and he should tell the purchaser to annul the sale, so that he can sell him the like of it or something better than it for less than that price. Purchase upon purchase is [also] forbidden, i.e. that he should tell the seller to annul the sale so that he can buy it for a higher price. Similarly, offering for sale on top of one's brother's offering for sale is forbidden. All of this enters into this hadith in order to elucidate the [full] meaning which is to hate each other and to turn the back on each other.

To restrict the prohibition to the sale of one's brother [by taking the word 'brother' in the sense of another Muslim] would require that it is not forbidden [to sell] on the sale of a *kafir*, which is a view of Ibn Khalwayh, but the correct position is that there is no difference [between a contract made with a Muslim or with a *kafir*], since it falls under fulfilling obligations and contracts.

By his ﷺ saying, "'*Taqwa* is here' and he pointed to his breast with his hand three times", he meant the heart. There has already been mentioned his ﷺ saying, "Certainly in the body there is a lump of flesh which when it is sound the whole body is sound...."[i]

His ﷺ saying, "...and he does not fail to assist him" i.e. upon his commanding the good and forbidding the wrong or upon his seeking one of his rights, rather he helps, aids and protects him from harm as much as he can.

His ﷺ saying, "...nor despise him" i.e. he does not judge that he is better than someone else, rather he should reckon that others are better than him or he should pass no judgement, because the end result is hidden and a slave does not know what the seal of his actions will be. If he sees a Muslim youth, he should reckon that he is better than him, considering the fact that he has less wrong actions than him. If he sees someone who is older than him, he should reckon him to be better than him, considering the fact that he emigrated before him in Islam. If he sees a *kafir* he should not pass judgement on him that he is certain to go to the Fire, because of the possibility that he will accept Islam and die as a Muslim.

His ﷺ saying, "It is sufficient evil for a man that he should despise his brother" meaning that this is a tremendous evil and that the punishment of this wrong action will suffice the perpetrator of it.

With respect to his ﷺ saying, "Every Muslim...", [we could

---

[i] See hadith number 6.

mention that] he ﷺ said on the Farewell Pilgrimage, "Your blood, your properties and your honour are sacred to you like the sanctity of this day of yours, in this month of yours, in this land of yours."[96] Al-Karabisi sought to show by this hadith that backbiting and attacking the honour of Muslims is a major wrong action,[i] either because of the indication given [here] by its being joined together with blood and wealth, or because of the comparison in his words, "...like the sanctity of this day of yours, in this month of yours, in this land of yours" for [the violation of] which Allah ﷻ has threatened a painful torment, when He ﷻ said, *"Those who desire to profane it (the haram of Makkah) with wrongdoing, We will let them taste a painful punishment."*[97]

---

[i] i.e. such as drinking alcohol, adultery, theft, unlawful killing, usury, etc.

الحديث السادس والثلاثون

عَنْ أَبِي هُرَيْرَةَ ﷺ عَنِ النَّبِيِّ ﷺ قَالَ:
مَنْ نَفَّسَ عَنْ مُؤْمِنٍ كُرْبَةً مِنْ كُرَبِ الدُّنْيَا نَفَّسَ اللَّهُ عَنْهُ كُرْبَةً مِنْ كُرَبِ يَوْمِ الْقِيَامَةِ، وَمَنْ يَسَّرَ عَلَى مُعْسِرٍ، يَسَّرَ اللَّهُ عَلَيْهِ فِي الدُّنْيَا وَالْآخِرَةِ، وَمَنْ سَتَرَ مُسْلِمًا سَتَرَهُ اللَّهُ فِي الدُّنْيَا وَالْآخِرَةِ، وَاللَّهُ فِي عَوْنِ الْعَبْدِ مَا كَانَ الْعَبْدُ فِي عَوْنِ أَخِيهِ، وَمَنْ سَلَكَ طَرِيقًا يَلْتَمِسُ فِيهِ عِلْمًا سَهَّلَ اللَّهُ لَهُ بِهِ طَرِيقًا إِلَى الْجَنَّةِ، وَمَا اجْتَمَعَ قَوْمٌ فِي بَيْتٍ مِنْ بُيُوتِ اللَّهِ يَتْلُونَ كِتَابَ اللَّهِ، وَيَتَدَارَسُونَهُ فِيمَا بَيْنَهُمْ؛ إِلَّا نَزَلَتْ عَلَيْهِمُ السَّكِينَةُ، وَغَشِيَتْهُمُ الرَّحْمَةُ، وَذَكَرَهُمُ اللَّهُ فِيمَنْ عِنْدَهُ، وَمَنْ أَبْطَأَ بِهِ عَمَلُهُ لَمْ يُسْرِعْ بِهِ نَسَبُهُ.

رَوَاهُ مُسْلِمٌ بِهَذَا اللَّفْظِ.

36. Easing Someone's Distress

Abu Hurairah ؓ narrated that the Prophet ﷺ said, "Whoever removes an anxiety of the world from a believer, Allah will remove an anxiety of the Day of Resurrection from him. Whoever makes it easy for someone in difficulty, Allah will make it easy for him in the world and the Next Life. Whoever conceals [the wrong action of] a Muslim, Allah will conceal his [wrong action] in the world and the Next Life. Allah will be of assistance to the slave as long as the slave is of assistance to his brother. Whoever travels on a path seeking in it knowledge, Allah will smooth for him a path by it to the Garden. People do not gather in one of the houses of Allah, reciting the Book of Allah, studying it together and teaching it to each other, but that tranquillity descends upon them, mercy covers them, the angels encircle them, and Allah remembers them among those who are with Him. Whoever's deeds hold him back will not be advanced by his lineage." Muslim narrated it in this wording.

Commentary

In his ﷺ saying, "Whoever removes an anxiety of the world from a believer, Allah will remove an anxiety of the Day of Rising from him", there is a proof that it is recommended to make [non-interest] loans [to people in difficulty], that it is recommended to free prisoners from the hands of disbelievers by wealth which one gives them, to free a Muslim from the hands of tyrants and to free him from prison. It is said that when Yusuf ؑ came out of the prison he wrote over its door, "This is the grave of the living, the malicious joy of one's enemies, and the testing of friends."

Undertaking to guarantee someone who is in financial difficulty is also included in this category, and standing surety in lieu of him, for someone who is able to do it. As for someone who lacks capacity, he must not do it. One of the companions of al-Qaffal said, "In the Tawrah it is written, 'Standing surety is blameworthy; the beginning of it is regret, the middle of it is blame, and the end of it is debt.'"

If it is said that Allah ﷻ says, *"Those who produce a good action will receive ten like it"*⁹⁸ and that this hadith shows that a good action is rewarded with the like of it, because it is rewarded with the removal of one anxiety of the Day of Resurrection and not ten, then the answer has two aspects. First, is that this is from the category of what is understood from a number (*mafhum al-'adad*),ⁱ and the judgement attached to a number does not show the negation of increase and decrease. Second, each distress of the Day of Resurrection comprises many terrors, difficult states, and abundant dangers, and these terrors are in excess of ten and multiples of it.

In the hadith there is another concealed secret which is made apparent by means of [elucidating] that which is inherent: there is a promise through the informing of the Truthful One ﷺ that whoever removes a Muslim's distress will have a good seal [on his life's actions] and that he will die in Islam, because disbelievers will not be shown mercy in the Abode of the Next Life and no distress will be removed from them. In the hadith there is an indication of the good news contained in the expression transmitted from the Owner of the Standard [on the Last Day], so in this tremendous promise let the trusting trust, *"It is for the like of this that all workers should work!"*⁹⁹

ⁱ *Mafhum al-'adad* is a type of *mafhum al-mukhalafah*, a term from *usul al-fiqh*. The immediate sense here is that if ten is mentioned it does not mean nine or eleven are ruled out. The Imam's position is that the number ten is not exact and is not meant to rule out the possibility of a lesser or greater number.

The best action is to remove distress, and in the hadith there is a proof that it is recommended to conceal [the wrong action of] a Muslim, if one discovers that he is doing something wrong. Allah ﷻ says, *"People who love to see filth being spread about concerning those who have iman will have a painful punishment both in the dunya and the akhirah."*[100] [Also] it is preferable if a human being does a wrong action, that he himself should conceal [it].

As for those who witness adultery there is disagreement about them in two ways, one of which is that it is preferable for them to conceal [the adultery], the second is that they should bear witness. Someone made a distinction and said, "If they see some benefit in bearing witness, then they should bear witness, and if [they see benefit] in concealing [the adultery] then they should conceal it."

In the hadith there is also a proof of the preferability of walking in search of knowledge. It is related that Allah ﷻ revealed to Dawud ﷺ, "Take hold of an iron staff and two iron sandals, and walk in search of knowledge until the sandals are torn and the staff is broken." In it also there is an indication that one should serve men of knowledge and cling to their company, travel with them and gain knowledge from them. Allah ﷻ says, in narrating about Musa ﷺ that he said [to Khidr], *"May I follow you on condition that you teach me some of the right guidance you have been taught?"*[101]

Know that this hadith has conditions, of which there is [that one must hold to] action according to what one knows. Anas ﷺ said, "The concern of men of knowledge is being mindful, the concern of fools is narration." The poet said:

> "The admonitions of the admonisher will not be accepted,
> until first of all his [own] heart keeps it in mind.
> O my people! Who is more wrongdoing than an admonisher
> who contradicts what he has said in public?
> He makes his goodness public among people,
> and opposes the Merciful when he is alone."

Another condition is to spread it. Allah ﷻ says, *"If a party from each group of them were to go out so they could increase their knowledge of the deen they would be able to notify their people when they returned to them."*¹⁰² It is narrated that Anas ﷺ said that the Prophet ﷺ said to his companions, "Shall I not inform you of the most generous of the generous, and I am the most generous of the children of Adam? The most generous of them after me is [first] a man who learns a science and then spreads it; Allah will raise him up on the Day of Resurrection as a nation by himself, and [second] a man who is generous with himself in the way of Allah until he is killed."¹⁰³

A condition is to give up boastful competitiveness and contentiousness. It is narrated that the Prophet ﷺ said, "Whoever seeks knowledge for four [reasons] enters the Fire: in order to compete boastfully with people of knowledge, or to dispute with fools, or to take property and wealth by it, or to turn people's faces towards him."¹⁰⁴

Another condition is to anticipate a reward [from Allah] for spreading it, and to give up being mean with it. Allah ﷻ says, *"Say, 'I do not ask you for any wage for it.'"*¹⁰⁵

A condition is not to be too proud to say, "I do not know." He ﷺ said even with the exaltedness of his degree, when he was asked about the Hour, "The one who is asked knows no more than the one who asks."ⁱ He was asked about the *Ruh* and he said, "I do not know."

A condition is self-abasement. Allah ﷻ says, *"The slaves of the All-Merciful are those who walk lightly on the earth."*¹⁰⁶ He ﷺ said to Abu Dharr, "Abu Dharr, bear in mind the advice of your Prophet; perhaps Allah will benefit you by it. Show humility towards Allah, mighty is He and majestic, perhaps He will raise you up by it on the Day of Resurrection. Greet whomever you meet of my

---

i   See hadith number 2.

Ummah, good or bad, dress yourself with coarse clothing, and do not want by that anything but the face of Allah ﷻ and perhaps pride and scorn will not find an entrance into your heart."

A condition is to bear in mind the possibility of harm [to oneself] in spreading good counsel, and modelling oneself on the right-acting first generations in all of that. Allah says, *"Command what is right and forbid what is wrong and be steadfast in the face of all that happens to you."*[107] He ﷺ said, "No prophet has suffered what I have suffered."[i]

A condition is that one should intend by one's knowledge [to give it to] the one who is in most need of teaching, just as one intends by *sadaqah* from one's wealth [to give it to] the most needy and then the most needy [after them], for whoever revives an ignorant person by teaching him knowledge is as if he had revived all people. One thing that has been said about awakening a neglectful person and making him return to obedience is:

"Whoever returns a fleeing slave who has taken fright,
Then the One who forgives will pardon his wrong action."

His ﷺ saying, "...but that tranquillity descends upon them" and *as-sakeenah* "tranquillity" is on the form *fa'eelah* of the word *sukun* "stillness", i.e. tranquillity from Allah. Allah ﷻ says, *"Only in the remembrance[ii] of Allah can the heart find peace,"*[108] and remembrance of Allah is sufficient honour, [i.e.] Allah's remembering the slave

---

[i] Abu Nu'aim related it in the *Hilyat al-Awliya*. It is sometimes wrongly thought from its title that the book of Abu Nu'aim is a series of biographies of Sufi saints. Rather it contains biographical outlines of the first generations of Muslims up until the author's own generation which he narrates by the criteria of the science of hadith. Thus it has biographies of both the Imams of *fiqh* and of early *salihun* such as Dhu'n-Nun al-Misri and Ibrahim ibn Adham. It is illustrative that we find Dhu'n-Nun to have been one who learnt the *Muwatta* by heart directly from Imam Malik.

[ii] *Dhikr* in Arabic means both "mention" and "remembrance", the former being outer and the latter inner. Allah says, *"Remember Me – I will remember you."* (Surat al-Baqarah: 151). *Dhikru'llah* – 'Remembrance of Allah' – is here taken to mean Allah's remembering the slave.

in the Highest Assembly, and for this reason it is said:
> "Be plentiful in remembrance of Him on earth, continuously,
> so that you might be remembered in heaven when you remember."

It has been said:
> "An hour of remembrance – know it! – is abundance and wealth,
> and an hour of distraction is bankruptcy and poverty."

His ﷺ saying, "Whoever's deeds hold him back", means that even if he has a noble lineage, his lineage will not hasten him to the Garden. The one who acts in obedience, even if he is an Abyssinian slave, has precedence over the inactive, even if he is a Qurayshi noble. Allah ﷻ says, *"The noblest among you in Allah's sight is the one with the most taqwa."*[i]

---

[i] Surat al-Hujurat: 13. 'Noblest' also means 'most generous'.

الحديث السابع والثلاثون

عَنْ ابْنِ عَبَّاسٍ رَضِيَ اللَّهُ عَنْهُمَا عَنْ رَسُولِ اللَّهِ ﷺ فِيمَا يَرْوِيهِ عَنْ رَبِّهِ تَبَارَكَ وَتَعَالَى، قَالَ:

إِنَّ اللَّهَ كَتَبَ الْحَسَنَاتِ وَالسَّيِّئَاتِ، ثُمَّ بَيَّنَ ذَلِكَ، فَمَنْ هَمَّ بِحَسَنَةٍ فَلَمْ يَعْمَلْهَا كَتَبَهَا اللَّهُ عِنْدَهُ حَسَنَةً كَامِلَةً، وَإِنْ هَمَّ بِهَا فَعَمِلَهَا كَتَبَهَا اللَّهُ عِنْدَهُ عَشْرَ حَسَنَاتٍ إِلَى سَبْعِمِائَةِ ضِعْفٍ إِلَى أَضْعَافٍ كَثِيرَةٍ، وَإِنْ هَمَّ بِسَيِّئَةٍ فَلَمْ يَعْمَلْهَا كَتَبَهَا اللَّهُ عِنْدَهُ حَسَنَةً كَامِلَةً، وَإِنْ هَمَّ بِهَا فَعَمِلَهَا كَتَبَهَا اللَّهُ سَيِّئَةً وَاحِدَةً.

رَوَاهُ الْبُخَارِيُّ، وَمُسْلِمٌ، فِي "صَحِيحَيْهِمَا" بِهَذِهِ الْحُرُوفِ.

37. Good and Bad Actions

Ibn 'Abbas ☙ narrated from the Messenger of Allah ﷺ in that which he related from his Lord, blessed is He and exalted, "Allah has written the good and bad actions, then He explained that. Whoever intends to do a good action but does not do it, Allah writes it down with Himself as a complete good action. If he intends to do it and does it, Allah writes it down with Himself as ten good actions, up to seven hundred multiples [of it], up to many multiples [of it]. If he intends to do a wrong action then does not do it, Allah writes it down with Himself as a complete good action. If he intends to do it and then does it, Allah writes it down as a single wrong action." Al-Bukhari and Muslim narrated it in their two *sahih* books exactly like this.

Look my brother – may Allah grant us grace and guide us and you to the vastness of the kindness of Allah ﷻ – and consider these words. His words "with Himself" indicate His taking trouble with it. His word "complete" is in order to lay stress on it, and to emphasise the strength of His concern for it. He said about the wrong action which he [the person] proposes to do and later abandons, "Allah writes it down with Himself as a complete good action" and he emphasised it with "complete". "And if he does it Allah writes it down as a single wrong action" and he laid stress on its littleness by the word "single" and he did not emphasise it with "complete". To Allah belongs the praise and the favour bestowed. We cannot enumerate His praise, and by Allah success is obtained.

Commentary

About his ﷺ saying, "Allah writes it down with Himself as ten good actions, up to seven hundred multiples [of it], up to many multiples [of it]", al-Bazzar narrated in his *Musnad* that he ﷺ said, "Actions are seven [types]: two actions which make obligatory, and two actions which are one for one, and an action the good of which is [rewarded] with ten, and an action the good of which is [rewarded] with seven hundred multiples, and an action whose reward none but Allah ﷻ can enumerate. As for the two actions which make obligatory, they are *kufr*[i] and *iman*. *Iman* makes the Garden obligatory and *kufr* makes the Fire obligatory. As for the two actions which are one for one, then whoever proposes to do a good action and does not do it, Allah writes it down for him as a good action, and whoever does a wrong action Allah writes it down against him as one wrong action. As for the action for which there is seven hundred multiples, it is the dirham [spent] in *jihad* in the way of Allah. Allah ﷻ says, "...*[like] a grain which produces seven ears; in every ear there are a hundred grains.*"[ii] Moreover, Allah ﷻ mentioned that He multiplies [rewards] for whomever He wills in excess of that, and He ﷻ said, "*...and if there is a good deed Allah will multiply it and pay out an immense reward direct from Him.*"[109] The *ayah* and hadith, i.e. his ﷺ words "up to many multiples" show that ten-fold up to seven hundred-fold are words which are not being used to limit [the reward], and that He will multiply [the reward] for whomever He wills, and give from Himself that which cannot be numbered or counted. Glory be to the One Whose favours cannot be enumerated and Whose blessings cannot be counted, and gratitude is owed to Him and blessing and bounty. As for the seventh it is fasting. Allah ﷻ says, "Every action of the son of Adam is for him except for fasting, for it is for Me and I will recompense it."[110] No-one knows the reward of fasting but Allah.[iii]

---

[i] *Kufr* is literally 'covering over' and also means 'ingratitude', 'disbelief' and 'rejection'.

[ii] Surat al-Baqarah: 261. "*The metaphor of those who spend their wealth in the Way of Allah is that of a grain which produces seven ears; in every ear there are a hundred grains.*"

[iii] Ibn Juzayy said, "It has been said that every good action has a limited reward, from ten-fold up to seven-hundred fold, except for patience whose reward has no limit. That is because of Allah's words, '*Only the patient are paid their reward without reckoning.*'" There is no contradiction here since patience is an intrinsic part of fasting and it has been said that fasting is an intrinsic part of patience.

الحديث الثامن والثلاثون

عَنْ أَبِي هُرَيْرَةَ ﷺ قَالَ: قَالَ رَسُولُ اللَّهِ ﷺ إِنَّ اللَّهَ تَعَالَى قَالَ: مَنْ عَادَى لِي وَلِيًّا فَقَدْ آذَنْتُهُ بِالْحَرْبِ، وَمَا تَقَرَّبَ إِلَيَّ عَبْدِي بِشَيْءٍ أَحَبَّ إِلَيَّ مِمَّا افْتَرَضْتُهُ عَلَيْهِ، وَلَا يَزَالُ عَبْدِي يَتَقَرَّبُ إِلَيَّ بِالنَّوَافِلِ حَتَّى أُحِبَّهُ، فَإِذَا أَحْبَبْتُهُ كُنْتُ سَمْعَهُ الَّذِي يَسْمَعُ بِهِ، وَبَصَرَهُ الَّذِي يُبْصِرُ بِهِ، وَيَدَهُ الَّتِي يَبْطِشُ بِهَا، وَرِجْلَهُ الَّتِي يَمْشِي بِهَا، وَلَئِنْ سَأَلَنِي لَأُعْطِيَنَّهُ، وَلَئِنِ اسْتَعَاذَنِي لَأُعِيذَنَّهُ.

رَوَاهُ الْبُخَارِيُّ.

38. Obligatory and Optional Acts and Wilayah

Abu Hurairah ﷺ said, "The Messenger of Allah ﷺ said, 'Allah ﷻ says, "Whoever shows enmity to a close friend of Mine, then I declare war on him. My slave does not draw closer to Me with anything more beloved to Me than that

THE COMPLETE FORTY HADITH

which I have made obligatory upon him. My slave continues to draw closer with optional extra acts until I love him. When I love him, I am his hearing with which he hears, his sight with which he sees, his hand with which he grasps and his foot with which he walks. If he asks Me I will definitely give him, and if he seeks refuge with Me I will definitely give him refuge.'"" Al-Bukhari narrated it.

Commentary

What is meant here by "close friend" in his ﷺ saying from his Lord ﷻ, "Whoever shows enmity to a close friend of Mine, then I declare war on him" is the *mu'min*. Allah ﷻ says, *"Allah is the protector (wali)*[i] *of those who have iman."*[111] Whoever harms a believer, then Allah announces war on him, i.e. Allah informs him that He is at war with him, and when Allah ﷻ wages war on a slave He destroys him, so let man beware of opposing any Muslim.

In His ﷻ saying, "My slave does not draw closer to Me with anything more beloved to Me than that which I have made obligatory upon him", there is proof that the performance of obligatory acts is better than optional extra acts. It has been narrated in the hadith literature that, "The reward of the obligatory is seventy times better than the reward of optional acts."[112]

About His ﷻ saying, "My slave continues to draw closer with optional extra acts until I love him", the people of knowledge ﵁ have made a simile. They have said that the simile of someone who performs extra optional acts along with the obligatory, and the simile of someone else, is a man who gives to one of his two slaves a dirham with which to buy fruit and gives to another

---

[i] The root of *wali* has the sense of closeness, friendship and protection, as well as giving rise to words to do with governance.

38. Optional Acts and Wilayah

a dirham with which to buy fruit. One of the two slaves went and bought fruit, then placed it in a fruit basket and, of his own volition, sprinkled on it some herbs and sweet smelling plants. Then he went and placed it before his master. The other went and bought fruit in the orchard, then came and placed it before his master on the ground. Each slave was obedient, but one of them, of his own volition, gave a fruit basket, herbs and sweet smelling plants and so became more beloved to the master. Whoever prays extra optional prayers[i] along with the obligatory prayers becomes more beloved to Allah. Love from Allah is [His] willing the best [for one]. Whenever He loves His slave He occupies him in His remembrance and obedience, He protects him from shaytan, He occupies his limbs in acts of obedience, He makes hearing the Qur'an and *dhikr* beloved to him and makes hearing singing and instruments of diversion detestable to him. He becomes one of those about whom Allah has said, *"When they hear worthless talk they turn away from it,"*[113] and [about whom] He ﷻ said, *"And, who, when the ignorant speak to them, say, 'Peace,'"*[114] i.e. if they hear some indecent talk from them they turn away from it, and they say something with which they are safe [from wrong action]. He guards his sight from those things which it is forbidden [to see] and he does not look at that which is not permitted for him, so his looking becomes a look of reflection and consideration, and he does not see anything which has been created but that he has a proof from it of its Creator. 'Ali ؇ said, "I do not see anything but that I see Allah ﷻ before it." The meaning of consideration is to pass, through reflection, from creations to the power of the

---

[i] The Imam uses the prayer as an illustration, but of course it can equally well be applied to all of the obligations, the ordinary transactions and to *jihad*. If anyone discharges his obligatory duties and then of his own volition freely gives more than that, whether it is *sadaqah*, extra fasting, extra Hajjs and 'Umrahs, or extra effort for the revival and establishment of the *deen*, he will come within the meaning contained in this hadith, and Allah knows best.

Creator, so that he glorifies [Allah] at that, declares His sanctity and vastness, the movements of his two hands and his feet all become for the sake of Allah ﷻ, he does not walk for a purpose which does not concern him, does not do anything profitless with his hand, rather his movements and stillnesses are all for Allah ﷻ and so he is rewarded for that in his movements, stillnesses and in all of his actions.

His ﷻ words, "I become his hearing..." may mean, "I am the One who protects his hearing and sight, the grasp of his hand, and his foot from shaytan" or it may be, "I am in his heart when he hears, sees and grasps, so when he remembers Me, he withholds himself from acting for other than Me."

الحديث التاسع والثلاثون

عَنْ ابْنِ عَبَّاسٍ رَضِيَ اللهُ عَنْهُمَا أَنَّ رَسُولَ اللهِ ﷺ قَالَ: إِنَّ اللهَ تَجَاوَزَ لِي عَنْ أُمَّتِي الْخَطَأَ وَالنِّسْيَانَ وَمَا اسْتُكْرِهُوا عَلَيْهِ.

حَدِيثٌ حَسَنٌ، رَوَاهُ ابْنُ مَاجَهْ، وَالْبَيْهَقِيّ.

39. Mistakes, Forgetfulness and Coercion

Ibn 'Abbas narrated that the Messenger of Allah said, "Allah has passed over, for my sake, my Ummah's mistakes and their forgetfulness and that which they are forced to do." A good hadith which Ibn Majah, al-Bayhaqi and others narrated.

Commentary

His saying, "Allah has passed over, for my sake, my Ummah's mistakes and their forgetfulness and that which they are forced to do" i.e. He passes over the guilt of their mistakes, forgetfulness and that which they are forced to do. As for the judgement on mistakes, forgetfulness and that which they are forced to do, it is not lifted, for even if something was destroyed by mistake or something entrusted to one was lost out of forgetfulness one is bound to honour the liability [one incurred]. Being forced to commit adultery and murder are both excluded [from being passed over by Allah, exalted is He], and they are not permitted through coercion.^i Excluded from forgetfulness is that which man takes hold the cause of, for he is guilty by doing it because of his shortcoming.^ii This hadith contains benefits and important matters about which I have compiled a work but which this book is not capable [of containing].^iii

---

^i They may not be forgiven even if done under compulsion. They involve not only the rights of Allah but the rights of the person who has been wronged.

^ii It means that if one becomes involved in something that one knows is going to cause one's forgetfulness of an obligation then one is not excused because of that forgetfulness. In modern Arabic it could be construed that it refers to taking substances that cause forgetfulness, but it is not certain that this was its meaning to the author.

^iii Contracts undertaken under coercion are not binding. An instance of this was that Imam Malik held very vigorously that a divorce pronounced under compulsion is not binding. He was forbidden by the Abbasid governor of Madinah from stating this publicly and when he continued to do so, he was humiliated and punished in public, but refused to recant. The governor and the people of Madinah all knew that a consequence of this judgement of Malik was that the oath of allegiance taken under compulsion was thus not binding.

الحديث الأربعون

عَنْ ابْنِ عُمَرَ رَضِيَ اللَّهُ عَنْهُمَا قَالَ: أَخَذَ رَسُولُ اللَّهِ ﷺ بِمَنْكِبِي، وَقَالَ:

كُنْ فِي الدُّنْيَا كَأَنَّكَ غَرِيبٌ أَوْ عَابِرُ سَبِيلٍ.

وَكَانَ ابْنُ عُمَرَ رَضِيَ اللَّهُ عَنْهُمَا يَقُولُ:

إِذَا أَمْسَيْتَ فَلَا تَنْتَظِرِ الصَّبَاحَ، وَإِذَا أَصْبَحْتَ فَلَا تَنْتَظِرِ الْمَسَاءَ، وَخُذْ مِنْ صِحَّتِكَ لِمَرَضِكَ، وَمِنْ حَيَاتِكَ لِمَوْتِكَ.

رَوَاهُ الْبُخَارِيُّ.

40. BE IN THE WORLD AS IF A STRANGER

Ibn 'Umar ﷺ said, "The Messenger of Allah ﷺ took hold of my shoulder and said, 'Be in the world as if you were a stranger or someone traversing a way.'" Ibn 'Umar ﷺ used to say, "When you enter upon the evening, do not expect the morning, and when you get up in the morning, do not await the evening, and take from your health for your sickness, and from your life for your death." Al-Bukhari narrated it.

Commentary

His ﷺ saying, "Be in the world as if you were a stranger or someone traversing a way" i.e. do not depend on it nor take it as your homeland, do not consider abiding in it nor become attached to any of it except that with which the stranger concerns himself when he is not in his own country and wants to leave it to return to his family. This is what Salman al-Farisi meant ﷺ when he said, "My intimate friend ﷺ told me that I must only take from the world as if it were the provisions of a rider."

Something said about doing-without in the world is:

"Do you build as those who live forever,
  and yet your staying in it, if you would only think, is little?
Certainly in the shade of the Arak trees there is sufficient
  for whomever is in it, and [then] the saddled camel comes to him [ready for departure]."

Another thing that is said about doing-without in the world:

"You hope to live forever in an abode which does not endure forever,
  and have you heard of a shadow which does not move?"

Another said:

"You are imprisoned in it and you love it!
How can you love that in which you are imprisoned?
Do not be distracted by an abode in which you are.
  It will separate you one day from that by which you were distracted.
It will feed you food, and soon
  it will give you the taste of that which you have been fed."[i]

In the hadith there is an indication [that one should] curtail one's wishful thinking, hasten to repentance and prepare for death. If a man wishes for something let him say, "If Allah wills" for Allah ﷻ says, *"Never say about anything, 'I am doing that tomorrow,' without adding 'If Allah wills.'"*[115]

---

[i] In Surat al-'Ankabut: 55, Allah ﷻ says, *"Taste what you were doing."*

40. Be in the World as if a Stranger

In his ﷺ saying, "Take from your health...", he ﷺ told him to take advantage of hours of health by doing right action in them, for he will be incapable of fasting and [optional] prayer, etc., for reasons which come with ill health and old age.[i]

In his ﷺ saying, "...and from your life for your death", he ﷺ told him to send provision on [for himself]. This is like His ﷺ saying, "*And let each self look to what it has sent forward for Tomorrow.*"[116] One should not overstep the bounds in it until death takes one and one says, "*My Lord, send me back again so that perhaps I may act rightly regarding the things I failed to do!*"[117] Al-Ghazali said, may Allah show him mercy, "The son of Adam's body is like the net with which he earns right actions, so that if he earns good and then dies, it [the good] suffices him and he no longer needs the net, i.e. the body from which he has parted by his death. There is no doubt that when man dies, his appetites are cut off from the world, and his self desires right action because it is the provision of the grave. If he has some, it is enough for him. If he has none, he seeks to return from it to the world to take provision from it. That is after the net has been taken away from him, so that it will be said to him, 'It is extremely improbable, because it has gone.' He will remain always bewildered, regretting his remissness in taking provision before the net was taken from him." For this reason the Messenger of Allah ﷺ said, "Take from your life for your death" and there is no power [to avert evil] nor strength [to do good] except by Allah the Exalted, the Vast.

---

[i] The sick person is permitted not to fast Ramadan but he will have to make it up later. However, frail old people may choose to feed people instead of fasting, and according to the Malikis they do not have to feed people. The obligatory prayer may never be abandoned even if one has to perform it lying down in a sickbed, but sickness may prevent one from extra acts of *'ibadah*.

الحديث الحادي والأربعون

عَنْ أَبِي مُحَمَّدٍ عَبْدِ اللَّهِ بْنِ عَمْرِو بْنِ الْعَاصِ رَضِيَ اللَّهُ عَنْهُمَا، قَالَ: قَالَ رَسُولُ اللَّهِ ﷺ:

لَا يُؤْمِنُ أَحَدُكُمْ حَتَّى يَكُونَ هَوَاهُ تَبَعًا لِمَا جِئْتُ بِهِ.

حَدِيثٌ حَسَنٌ صَحِيحٌ، رَوَيْنَاهُ فِي كِتَابِ "الْحُجَّةِ" بِإِسْنَادٍ صَحِيحٍ.

41. NONE OF YOU BELIEVES UNTIL...

Abu Muhammad 'Abdullah[i] ibn 'Amr ibn al-'As ﷺ said, "The Messenger of Allah ﷺ said, 'None of you believes until his desire follows that with which I have come.'" A good *sahih* hadith which we have narrated in the book *al-Hujjah* with a *sahih isnad*.

Commentary

His ﷺ saying, "None of you believes until his desire follows

---

[i] 'Abdullah was one of the great Companions. He was one of their men of knowledge and he did without the world and fasted and prayed a great deal more than the obligatory fasts and prayers. He was one of those who memorised most from the Messenger of Allah ﷺ and thus who narrated the most hadith – 700. He was with his father, 'Amr ibn al-'As, until his father died in Egypt, and then he moved to Sham, then to Makkah. He became blind in later years. He died in Makkah in 65 AH at seventy-two years of age.

41. None of You Believes until...

that with which I have come", means that a person must measure his conduct by the Book and Sunnah, and he must oppose his own desire and follow that which the Messenger of Allah ﷺ brought. This is the equivalent of His ﷻ words, *"When Allah and His Messenger have decided something it is not for any mu'min man or woman to have a choice about it."*[118] No one along with Allah ﷻ and His Messenger ﷺ has command nor desire.

Ibrahim ibn Muhammad al-Kufi said, "I saw ash-Shafi'i in Makkah giving legal judgements to people, and I saw Ishaq ibn Rahwayh and Ahmad ibn Hanbal present there. Ahmad said to Ishaq, 'Come along, so that I can show you a man the like of whom your eyes have never seen.' Ishaq said to him, 'The like of whom my eyes have never seen?' He said, 'Yes,' and brought him to stand in front of ash-Shafi'i" and he told the story up until the point where he said, "Then Ishaq went on to the assembly of ash-Shafi'i and asked him about renting houses in Makkah,[i] and ash-Shafi'i said, "This is permissible according to us. The Messenger of Allah ﷺ said, 'Has 'Aqil left us a house?' Ishaq said, 'Yazid ibn Harun told us from Hisham from al-Hasan that that was not his view, and 'Ata and Tawus did not hold that view.' Ash-Shafi'i said, 'Are you the one about whom the people of Khurasan claim that you are their *faqih*?' Ishaq said, 'So they claim.' Ash-Shafi'i said, 'How much I would like that someone other than you should stand in your place. I would order that his ears should be rubbed [because he does not hear properly]. I say, "The Messenger of Allah ﷺ said" and you say, "'Ata, Tawus, al-Hasan and Ibrahim did not have that opinion?"[ii] Does anyone have an argument with

---

[i] The crux of the argument is whether the people of Makkah truly are the owners of their houses and thus free to rent them out and sell them, etc. Ash-Shafi'i showed that, in the texts he quotes, the ownership clearly belongs to them and thus they must be free to rent their own houses out.

[ii] In some cases, however, the early *fuqaha'* held that the view of a contemporary *faqih* or body of *fuqaha'* was a better proof of the Sunnah of

the Messenger of Allah ﷺ?' Then ash-Shafi'i said, 'Allah ﷻ says, "*It is for the poor of the Muhajirun who were driven from their homes*"[119] and are the homes attributed to owners or to someone other than owners?' Ishaq said, 'To owners.' Ash-Shafi'i said, 'Then the word of Allah ﷻ is the truest of words, and the Messenger of Allah ﷺ said, 'Whoever enters the house of Abu Sufyan is safe' and 'Umar ibn al-Khattab ؓ bought the House of the Two Alcoves [or chambers].' Ash-Shafi'i mentioned many groups of the Companions of the Messenger of Allah ﷺ. Ishaq said to him, '... *equally for those who live near it and those who come from far away*'[120] and ash-Shafi'i said, 'What is meant by that is the Mosque [of Makkah] especially, which is that which is around the Ka'bah. If it had been as you claim, it would not have been permissible for anyone to seek his stray [camel] among the houses of Makkah, nor to confine the sacrificial animals, nor to drop dung, but however this pertains to the Mosque especially.' Ishaq was silent and did not speak, so ash-Shafi'i stopped speaking to him."

---

the Messenger of Allah ﷺ than some of the hadith. One of the strongest of the Madinan principles of *fiqh* is that the agreement of the people of Madinah of the Companions, Followers and Followers of the Followers as shown in their practice is a more sure evidence of the Sunnah than are hadith, more sure even than some of those we know as *sahih* hadith. They encapsulated this perspective in the saying, "One thousand narrating from one thousand is more sure than one narrating from one." The 'one thousand' is the transmission of the Sunnah in practice and in knowledge by the people of Madinah of the first generations. 'One from one' is the narration of hadith by hadith scholars. The *fuqaha* of Madinah would sometimes quote a hadith and then pass a judgement which contradicted it, doing that in order to demonstrate that they had not passed their judgement in ignorance of the hadith. There are instances of this in the *Muwatta*' of Imam Malik, which can be very surprising to modern Muslims. For the most thorough exposition of this see *Root Islamic Education* by Shaykh Abdalqadir as-Sufi.

الحديث الثاني والأربعون

عَنْ أَنَسِ بْنِ مَالِكٍ ﷺ قَالَ: سَمِعْتُ رَسُولَ اللَّهِ ﷺ يَقُولُ: قَالَ اللَّهُ تَعَالَى:

يَا ابْنَ آدَمَ إِنَّكَ مَا دَعَوْتَنِي وَرَجَوْتَنِي غَفَرْتُ لَكَ عَلَى مَا كَانَ مِنْكَ وَلَا أُبَالِي، يَا ابْنَ آدَمَ لَوْ بَلَغَتْ ذُنُوبُكَ عَنَانَ السَّمَاءِ ثُمَّ اسْتَغْفَرْتَنِي غَفَرْتُ لَكَ، يَا ابْنَ آدَمَ إِنَّكَ لَوْ أَتَيْتَنِي بِقُرَابِ الْأَرْضِ خَطَايَا ثُمَّ لَقِيتَنِي لَا تُشْرِكُ بِي شَيْئًا لَأَتَيْتُكَ بِقُرَابِهَا مَغْفِرَةً.

رَوَاهُ التِّرْمِذِيُّ، وَقَالَ: حَدِيثٌ حَسَنٌ صَحِيحٌ.

42. O Son of Adam

Anas ﷺ said, "I heard the Messenger of Allah ﷺ saying, 'Allah ﷻ says, "Son of Adam, as long as you call on Me and hope in Me, I will forgive whatever comes from you [of wrong actions] and I do not care. Son of Adam, even if your wrong actions were to reach to the clouds of the sky and then you were to seek forgiveness of Me I would forgive you.

Son of Adam, even if you were to come to Me with nearly the earth in wrong actions and then later you were to meet Me, not associating anything with Me, then I would definitely bring you nearly as much as it [the earth] in forgiveness.'"' At-Tirmidhi narrated it and said, "A good *sahih* hadith."

Commentary

In His ﷻ saying, "The clouds (*'anan*) of the sky", *'anan* is with a *fathah* (a) on the *'ayn* which is without a diacritical point, and it is said that it is 'clouds' and it is said that it is that of it which *'anna* [is apparent] to you, i.e. 'is apparent' when you raise your head.

His ﷻ saying, "And then you seek forgiveness of Me, I will forgive you" is the equal of His ﷻ saying, "*Anyone who does evil or wrongs himself and then asks Allah's forgiveness will find Allah Ever-Forgiving, Most Merciful.*"[121] Seeking forgiveness must be accompanied by turning [to Allah in repentance from the wrong action]. Allah ﷻ says, "*Ask your Lord for forgiveness and then make tawbah to Him,*"[122] and He said, "*Turn to Allah every one of you, mu'minun, so that hopefully you will have success.*"[123]

Know that the meaning of *istighfar* is seeking forgiveness, and that is the seeking forgiveness done by the people of wrong action. One may also seek forgiveness for a shortcoming in showing gratitude and that is the seeking forgiveness of close friends [of Allah] and people of right action. It may also be for neither of those reasons but purely out of gratitude and that was his ﷺ seeking forgiveness and the seeking forgiveness of the prophets, on them the blessings of Allah and His peace.

He ﷺ said, "The master [supplication for] seeking forgiveness is:

42. O Son of Adam

اللَّهُمَّ أَنْتَ رَبِّي لَا إلهَ إِلَّا أَنْتَ خَلَقْتَنِي وَأَنَا عَبْدُكَ وَأَنَا عَلَى عَهْدِكَ وَوَعْدِكَ مَا اسْتَطَعْتُ أَعُوذُ بِكَ مِنْ شَرِّ مَا صَنَعْتُ أَبُوءُ لَكَ بِنِعْمَتِكَ عَلَيَّ وَأَبُوءُ لَكَ بِذَنْبِي فَاغْفِرْ لِي فَإِنَّهُ لَايَغْفِرُ الذُّنُوبَ إِلَّا أَنْتَ

'O Allah, You are my Lord, there is no god but You. You created me and I am Your slave and I am upon Your contract and Your promise as much as I am able. I seek refuge with You from the evil that I have done. I acknowledge to You Your blessing upon me and I acknowledge my wrong action, so forgive me, for no one forgives wrong actions except for You.'" He ﷺ said to Abu Bakr ؓ: "Say:

اللَّهُمَّ إِنِّي ظَلَمْتُ نَفْسِي ظُلْماً كَثِيراً - وفي رواية ظُلْماً كَبِيراً - وَإِنَّهُ لَا يَغْفِرُ الذُّنُوبَ إِلَّا أَنْتَ فَاغْفِرْ لِي مَغْفِرَةً مِنْ عِنْدِكَ وَارْحَمْنِي إِنَّكَ أَنْتَ الْغَفُورُ الرَّحِيمُ

'O Allah, I have wronged myself with much injustice,' – and in another version 'great injustice' – 'and no one forgives wrong actions but You, so forgive me with a forgiveness from Yourself, and show mercy to me, truly You are the All-Forgiving, the Most Merciful.'"[124]

Endnotes

1. Surat al-Fath: 2.
2. Ibn Majah, Ibn Khuzaymah and al-Bayhaqi narrated it. Ibn Majah narrated it (among the) trustworthy.
3. Surat al-Hashr: 23.
4. Al-Bukhari and Muslim narrated it.
5. Al-Bukhari and Muslim narrated it.
6. Al-Bukhari and Muslim narrated it.
7. Surat al-'Ankabut: 29.
8. Surat al-Qasas: 20.
9. Surat ar-Rum: 9.
10. Surat al-Baqarah: 198.
11. Al-Bukhari and Muslim narrated it.
12. Surat an-Nisa: 34.
13. Surat al-Hujurat: 14.
14. Surat adh-Dhariyat: 35.
15. Surat al-Baqarah: 140.
16. Surat ash-Shura: 42.
17. Surat adh-Dhariyat: 9.
18. Surat ar-Ra'd: 39.
19. Surat al-Falaq: 1-2.
20. Abu Dawud related it.
21. Surah Luqman: 34.
22. Surat al-A'raf: 187.
23. Surat al-Ahzab: 63.
24. Al-Bukhari and Muslim narrated it.
25. Al-Bayhaqi narrated it from Ibn 'Umar.
26. Surat at-Tawbah: 109.
27. Agreed upon.
28. Surat at-Tariq: 6.
29. Surah Al 'Imran: 6.
30. Surat al-Kahf: 30.
31. Surat adh-Dhariyat: 23.
32. Surat at-Taghabun: 7.
33. Surah Ali 'Imran: 112.
34. Narrated by al-Bukhari and Muslim.
35. Al-Bayhaqi narrated it in *Shu'ab al-Iman*.
36. Surat an-Nahl: 43.
37. Surat at-Tawbah: 122.
38. Part of a hadith narrated by al-Bukhari and Muslim.
39. Surah Ali 'Imran: 98.
40. Surat al-Ma'idah: 101.
41. Surah Ta-Ha: 4.
42. Surat al-Muminun: 52.
43. Surat al-Baqarah: 171.
44. Surat al-Baqarah: 267.

45 Surat al-Kahf: 62.
46 Surat al-A'raf: 14.
47 Ibn Hibban narrated it in his *Sahih*.
48 Al-Bukhari and Muslim narrated it.
49 Surat al-Ahzab: 65.
50 At-Tirmidhi narrated it.
51 At-Tabarani narrated it with two *isnads* one of which is *sahih*.
52 Abu Dawud narrated it.
53 Abu Dawud narrated it.
54 Surat al-Mujadalah: 7.
55 Abu Dawud and at-Tirmidhi narrated it and at-Tirmidhi said, "Good, *sahih*."
56 Surat al-Hashr: 18.
57 Abu Ya'la and al-Bazzar related it.
58 Ibn Hibban narrated it.
59 'Abd ar-Razzaq narrated it in his book.
60 Al-Bayhaqi narrated it.
61 At-Tabarani narrated it in *al-Awsat*.
62 Surat al-Qalam: 4.
63 Surat an-Nahl: 97.
64 Surat ash-Shura: 30.
65 Surat as-Saffat: 143.
66 Surah Yunus: 91.
67 Surah Yunus: 107.
68 Surat al-Qasas: 33.
69 Surah Ta-Ha: 44.
70 Surat an-Nisā': 70.
71 Surat al-Baqarah: 194.
72 Surah Hud: 112.
73 Surah Fussilat: 31.
74 Ibid.
75 Ibid.
76 Muslim narrated it.
77 Surat al-Isra: 31.
78 Surat al-Ma'idah: 19.
79 Surat al-Furqan: 2.
80 Surat al-Isra: 111.
81 Ahmad and Abu Dawud narrated it.
82 Ahmad and Abu Ya'la narrated it.
83 Surat al-Baqarah: 177.
84 Surat as-Saff: 3.
85 Surat ar-Ra'd: 23.
86 Surah Ali 'Imran: 14.
87 Surat al-Furqan: 67.
88 At-Tabarani narrated it in *al-Awsat*.
89 Al-Bukhari and Muslim narrated it.
90 Surat at-Tawbah: 74.
91 Surat al-An'am: 23.
92 Surah Ali 'Imran: 76.
93 Surah Luqman: 17.
94 Surat al-Furqan: 72.
95 Malik, al-Bukhari, Muslim, at-Tirmidhi and Abu Dawud narrated it.
96 Al-Bukhari and Muslim narrated it.
97 Surat al-Hajj: 25.
98 Surat al-An'am: 160.
99 Surat as-Saffat: 61.
100 Surat an-Nur: 19.
101 Surat al-Kahf: 66.
102 Surat at-Tawbah: 122.
103 Abu Ya'la and al-Bayhaqi narrated it.
104 Ibn Majah narrated it.
105 Surat al-An'am: 90.
106 Surat al-Furqan: 63.
107 Surah Luqman: 17.
108 Surat ar-Ra'd: 28.

Endnotes

109	Surat an-Nisa: 40.	119	Surat al-Hashr: 8.
110	Al-Bukhari narrated it.	120	Surat al-Hajj: 25.
111	Surat al-Baqarah: 257.	121	Surat an-Nisā': 110.
112	Ibn Khuzaymah narrated it.	122	Surah Hud: 2.
113	Surat al-Qasas: 55.	123	Surat an-Nur: 31.
114	Surat al-Furqan: 63.	124	Ahmad, al-Bukhari and Muslim, at-Tirmidhi, an-Nasa'i and Ibn Majah from Ibn 'Umar and from Abu Bakr.
115	Surat al-Kahf: 23.		
116	Surat al-Hashr: 17.		
117	Surat al-Muminun: 99.		
118	Surat al-Ahzab: 36.		